THE GOLF SECRET

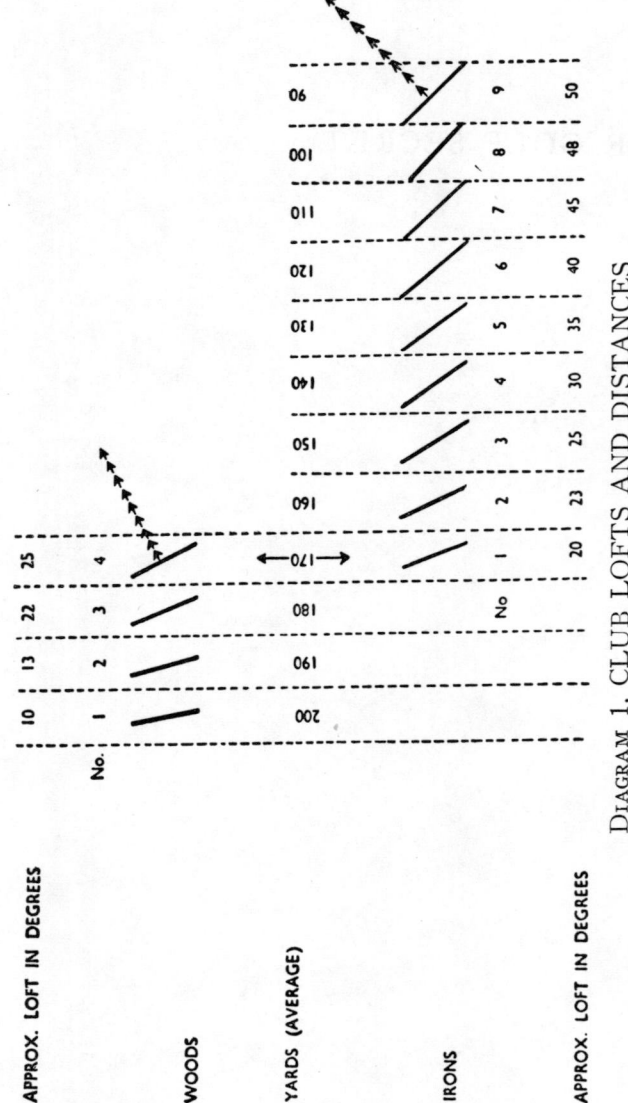

DIAGRAM 1. CLUB LOFTS AND DISTANCES

ARROWS REPRESENT FLIGHT OF BALL, AT RIGHT ANGLES TO CLUB FACE

The GOLF SECRET

by
H. A. MURRAY, M.D.

Preface by
ALGY EASTERBROOK

EMERSON BOOKS, INC. *New York*

COPYRIGHT, 1954, BY EMERSON BOOKS, INC.
Library of Congress Catalog Card Number 53-11154
Standard Book Number: 87523-093-8

SECOND EDITION, REVISED

Seventh Printing, April 1971

Manufactured in the United States of America

*This book is dedicated to the memory of
my great friend the late*
ISADORE SAMUELS
who first aroused my interest in golf

PUBLISHERS' NOTE

The warm and enthusiastic reception that greeted publication of the first edition of *The Golf Secret* makes possible this second, improved edition of Dr. Murray's excellent work. The publishers are gratified that their original estimate of the book as a major contribution to better golf has thus been generously confirmed by the golfers themselves, amateurs and pros.

When the author, a medical doctor as well as an avid golfer, set out to study the golf swing, his professional knowledge of how the body works led him to approach the game from an entirely new angle. His findings developed into *The Golf Secret*.

The publishers believe that Dr. Murray's clear exposition of the elements of the swing will provide . . . for duffers, for amateurs, and for pros . . . the "secret" of better golf.

bbb4107, 100_0119_0046

PREFACE

Having been for thirty-two years a golf professional, I did not think I could learn anything from a golf book, but after having read *The Golf Secret,* I have to confess that I have learned a great deal.

I have known Dr. Murray for eighteen years and have known of his analytical approach to golf, so that when he asked me to consider writing the preface to his book, I felt sure the book would be interesting if nothing more. It is much more!

He has apparently shown us professionals what we do and how we do it, by proving what happens to us all during the course of the swing; even though we ourselves hold many divergent views on this subject.

I have read many golf books that purported to show the easy way to play golf, and for years have endeavored to teach the game in the simplest way, but I have never seen the golf swing described, or thought of it, in so simple and straightforward a manner as in this book.

The author has carefully analyzed the golf swing and the factors that put it into a groove, thus simplifying its cultivation. He also appears to have proved that most of the movements of the golf swing (so interminably described and contradicted in other books) occur automatically and subconsciously.

I honestly think he has *hit the nail on the head.* It will certainly be easier to learn by his methods.

By following the principles suggested in this book, I believe that the ordinary golfer will acquire a reliable swing that will stand him in good stead, better than the swings described by many leading players, which are based on what each of them believes to be his own particular game.

It is my considered opinion that every golfer should read this book. The amount of information it contains is incredible. The anatomical information, as applied to golf—which I am sure has never before been published—is worth the price of the book. It explains much that we did not fully understand and shows golf from an entirely new angle.

I feel sure that none will read *The Golf Secret* without improvement in his playing and knowledge of the game.

Dr. Murray has done a great service to the game of golf and to all golfers. I congratulate him. I do not need to wish this book success—that is inevitable.

ALGY EASTERBROOK

CONTENTS

INTRODUCTION	xiii
1. THE GOLF SECRET—FIRST FACTOR	17
SHAPE OF THE BODY	
LENGTH OF CLUB SHAFT	
BODY MOVEMENTS	
ANGLES OF ADDRESS	
FUNCTION OF SPINE	
UPRIGHT AND FLAT SWINGS	
THE FEEL OF THE GOLF SWING	
THE CORRECT ATTITUDE	
2. THE GOLF SECRET—SECOND FACTOR	39
THE LEFT SHOULDER	
THE GOLF SWING WHEEL	
BACKSWING—FIRST MOVEMENT, DIRECTION OF LEFT-SHOULDER MOVEMENT, EXPERT CONFIRMATION, EXPERTS' CONTRADICTORY BELIEFS, EFFECTS OF CORRECT LEFT-SHOULDER MOVEMENT	
FORWARD SWING—FIRST MOVEMENT, DIRECTION OF LEFT-SHOULDER MOVEMENT, SPEED OF SHOULDER MOVEMENT, LIKELY MISGIVINGS, EXPERT CONFIRMATION, EXPERTS' CONTRADICTORY BELIEFS, EFFECTS OF CORRECT LEFT-SHOULDER MOVEMENT, CONVINCE YOURSELF	
LIMBER-UP	
3. THE GOLF SECRET—THIRD FACTOR	63
VOLUNTARY USE OF ARMS	
CHOICE OF METHOD	

CONTENTS

    DIRECTION OF ARM SWING
    EXPERT CONFIRMATION
    HOW TO DO IT
    SHORT SHOTS

4. THE GOLF SECRET—IN TRUE LIGHT   85
    USE AND MISUSE OF—
        WORDS—BACKSWING, DOWNSWING, HITTING DOWN, FOLLOW-THROUGH
        THE MIND—RELAXATION, CONCENTRATION
        THE BODY—SHAPE OF THE BODY, SHAPE OF THE SWING, BACKSWING, FORWARD SWING, INSIDE-TO-OUT FORWARD SWING, PRESSING, THE STOP AT THE TOP, TIMING, GOLF EXERCISES
        THE HEAD—EYE-ON-THE-BALL, HEAD-TURNING, HEAD-STILL, HEAD-DOWN, HEAD-UP, TOPPING, SLICING
        THE LEGS AND FEET—THE SET, THE FORWARD PRESS, THE PIVOT, LEFT-HEEL-RAISING, WEIGHT TRANSFERENCE, BALANCE, LEFT-HIP-BACK, LEFT-SIDE-OUT-OF-THE-WAY, LEFT-HEEL-DOWN, FIRM-LEFT-LEG
        THE ARMS—RIGHT-ELBOW-DOWN, STRAIGHT-LEFT-ARM, BACKSWING, HITTING DOWN WITH IRONS, PULL-DOWN-WITH-LEFT-ARM, HITTING LATE
        THE HANDS—WRISTS AND HANDS, LOOSE GRIP, WRIST-COCKING, WRIST-UNCOCKING, WRIST ROLL, OPEN FACE AND SHUT FACE, SCOOPING, WRIST FLICK, HITTING LATE, HITTING ENTIRELY WITH THE RIGHT HAND, PULL-DOWN-WITH-THE-LEFT-HAND, SNATCHING, HANDS-FIRST, SWING-STRAIGHT-BACK, CLUB-HEAD-CLOSE-TO-THE-GROUND, SWAYING
        THE FAIRWAY—DIVOTS AND BALL POSITION

5. Coordination of the Three Factors—with Other Details   141
    SHAPE OF THE BODY
    FEEL OF THE SWING
    BACKSWING
    FORWARD SWING
    POSTSCRIPT
    QUINTESSENCE

Index   157

DIAGRAMS

1.	Club Lofts and Distances	Frontispiece
2.	Face the Ball	18
3.	Back-bending	19
4.	Silhouettes of Experts	21
5.	Angles of Address	27
6.	The Golf Swing Wheel	43
7.	The Flattened Arc	50
8.	The Shoulder Angles	57
9.	The Three Hubs and the Three Arcs	64
10.	The Shoulder Swing	69
11.	The Arcs (Overhead View)	72
12.	Fastest Club-head Speed	75
13.	Divots	135
14.	Backspin	137

INTRODUCTION

Golf, as played by the leading professionals of today, is played the correct way, but the professionals have, as a body, failed to tell would-be golfers how to do it. Why? Presumably because they do not know what they do. Subsequently, I quote twelve leading players on starting the backswing, and twelve on the forward swing. In each instance they give twelve different versions. Since these two movements are universally admitted to be the very essence of golf, there can be no doubt about the truth of my indictment.

What chance has the unfortunate pupil-golfer of succeeding? Maybe he takes a lesson, or six lessons, or a dozen. He swings, and swings, and swings, until his hands are sore and blistered—which is often due to the loose grip he has been told to use. Still the ball won't go straight, so he reads another book, which probably makes matters worse because he tries to copy the intermediate positions depicted in the photographs. I have discovered that these intermediate positions, such as the middle of the backswing, are not voluntarily gone into. To deliberately swing into them will always produce a faulty swing. But more of that later.

Our learner will then probably accept a tip from a friend (or from a professional, as I have done on many occasions), which, at the time, appears to help him. But soon another fault appears, requiring further advice.

So it goes on, month after month, year after year, always patching and tinkering.

Regarding golf books—not to mention magazine and newspaper articles—I think that during the last eighteen years I must have read almost every one published and tried all the many methods they advocated. Although recently I have lost faith in golf books, I must admit that I have learned a lot from them, but chiefly from *really* studying the photographs and finding there much that was not pointed out by the authors. Many of these books are full of beautiful photographs, with captions purporting to describe what has taken place but rarely explaining how it happened or was done. For example, I have often read such statements as: "You can see the left hand is in control," "You can see the light right-hand grip," "You can see I am hitting downward," "You can see all the weight is on the right (or left) leg." I could go on indefinitely, but the point is that neither I nor anyone else can see any of those things. In fact, sometimes I think I can see just the opposite. The truth is that the writer is often "seeing" in the photographs what *he* does, or even more likely, what he thinks he does. Golf literature is notoriously contradictory!

It has been said that only twenty per cent of all who play golf can go around in less than ninety, and that only that twenty per cent are entitled to call themselves golfers. Just imagine! Eighty out of every hundred who play golf are duffers. I hope they will all buy this book and graduate to the other category.

There must be some reason for so much bad golf and for intelligent people's inability to knock a stationary ball in a straight line. It is not lack of enthusiasm, as every golfer—and his wife—knows.

There must be *something* that all professionals do, which they are unable to pass on.

Although there are slight differences, and maybe peculiarities, in professionals' setup and action, they all swing, basically, the same way. Presumably this is the much talked-of grooved swing. But how is it done? My studies, experiments, and observations have provided the answer to that.

There are lots of theories about golf, but hitherto there has been no real, universal, acceptable golf theory. Nothing, as there is in other professions, that you could set about learning with the certainty that it was right and would work. Producing just that was the task I set myself. Let me emphasize that it did not entail discovering a new method of playing golf, but merely finding out what the professionals do, and how they do it: avoiding the idiosyncrasies and eccentricities and finding the common denominator. That is what I claim to have done.

During my investigations, I have come to the conclusion that all professionals are right in some of the things they teach, but none of them knows all the answers. For example, some are right in demanding a firm or very firm grip; others are right in allowing the head to *turn* soon after impact; and others are right in stressing the importance of a ninety-degree shoulder turn on the backswing when playing a full shot. Others, who disagree with these precepts—in my view—are wrong.

Most of my contentions are supported by someone in authority or by some detail in their photographs. I have deliberately avoided the use of photographs because I am sure that they lead most people astray by encouraging them to try to assume the sequence of positions portrayed, which are really quite incidental to a correctly executed swing. Instead, I have drawn several diagrams that more precisely show my meaning.

I would like to acknowledge my indebtedness to Algy Easterbrook for many inspirations and also for consenting to write the preface—"if the manuscript proved acceptable to him."

After reading this book you will be able, in fewer weeks than it took me years, to "swing in the groove" and knock the ball straight and far, quite easily, with certainty, and without the many do's and don'ts normally required. You will be able to by-pass the many mistakes that I have made—and practiced—during many years, but you will also be deprived of the pleasure of profiting by your mistakes. Perhaps you would prefer to profit by mine!

H.A.M.

Chapter 1

THE GOLF SECRET—FIRST FACTOR

*Shape of the Body
Length of Club Shaft
Body Movements
Angles of Address
Function of Spine
Upright and Flat Swings
The Feel of the Golf Swing
The Correct Attitude*

SHAPE OF THE BODY

The first thing to realize when playing golf is that the ball to be hit is on the ground. This is not such a stupid observation as it may seem. I have watched hundreds of golfers who apparently don't realize it, or at any rate do not appreciate the importance of bending their bodies to face the ball. They stand almost erect with arms stuck forward, looking down their noses at the ball—the attitude in which they could best strike a ball off a post a few feet above the ground.

Visualize yourself hitting a ball located chest high on the face of a wall. You would not lie on your back but would stand erect—*i.e.,* you would face the ball. Now visualize the ball on the ground (the plane of which is of course ninety degrees to the wall), and you will see why you should not stand erect when playing golf but should bend your back—*i.e.,* why you should face the ball.

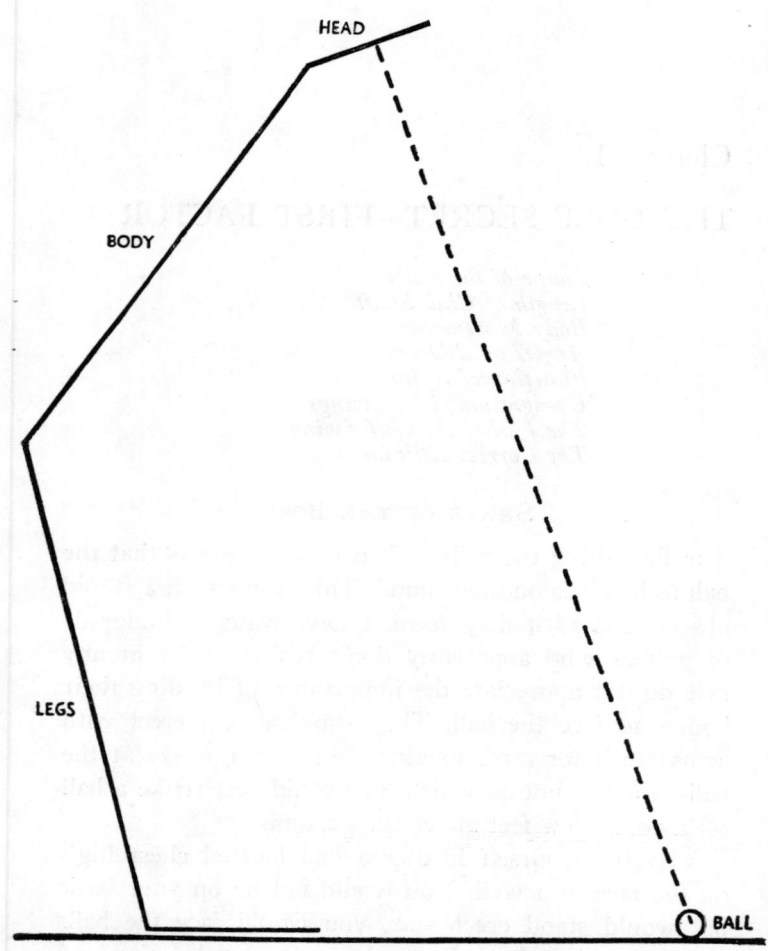

DIAGRAM 2. FACE THE BALL

Don't look down your nose at the ball. At the address, your eyes should be wide open, which they can be only if your face faces downward to the ball. Remember that the ball is on the ground, not in the air—*i.e.,* under you rather than in front of you. Your face and chest will then be approximately at right angles to a line connecting them with the ball.

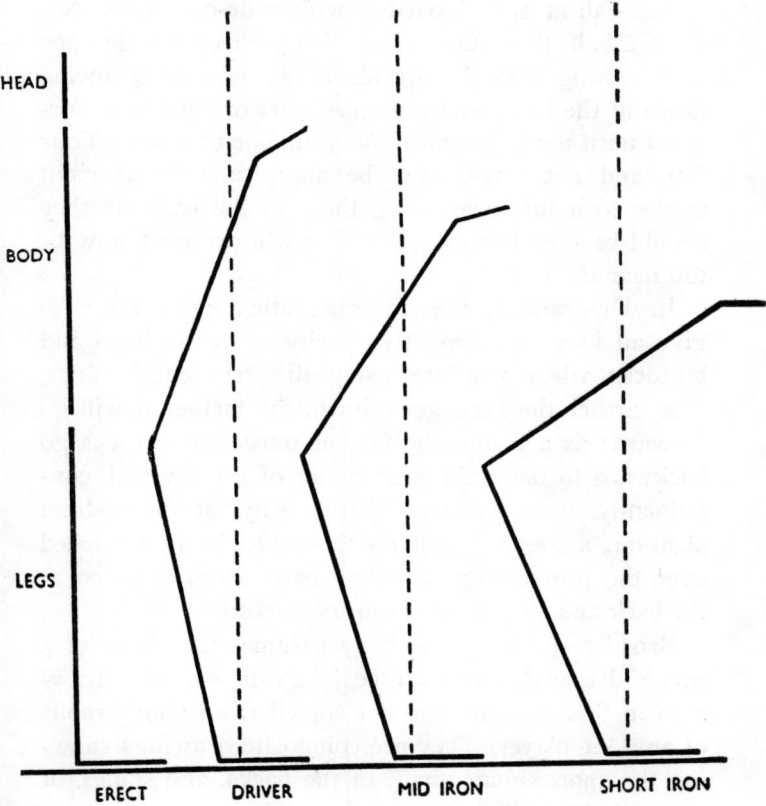

DIAGRAM 3. BACK-BENDING

DOTTED LINE—CENTER OF GRAVITY

Note the relative positions of head and buttocks when clubs of different lengths are used. With any golf stroke the body is far from the normal erect standing position; and as the club becomes shorter, the head and shoulders go forward and downward, while the buttocks go backward. Thus you maintain your center of gravity and, consequently, your balance.

The ball must be looked at with wide-open eyes. Address a ball, then stand erect with your eyes wide open and looking straight ahead. Now, without glancing down at the ball, bend the upper part of your body forward until the ball comes into your line of vision. Your face and chest will now be approximately at right angles to a line connecting them to the ball—as they should be (see Diagram 2). You will probably now be too near the ball.

In Diagram 3, the diagrammatic angles serve to give an idea of the relative positions of the head and buttocks when you are using different-length clubs. The farther the head goes down, the farther it will go forward; as a result, the farther must the buttocks go backward to maintain your center of gravity and, consequently, your balance. That is why, at the address position, an expert golfer's trousers (being stretched over the protruding buttocks) hang straight down at the back and cling to the front of the thighs.

Broadly speaking, the body assumes the shape of a reversed question mark (see Diagram 4). The drawings in this diagram are not copied from photographs of any one player. They are composite drawings showing the approximate shape of the backs, and spines, of most of the world's best golfers. The reader can confirm this by studying photographs in many golf books.

There are individual variations of back- and leg-bending, but most conform, more or less, to our Diagram 4.

When studying the leg-bending, the reader should remember that the actual shape of the legs is some-

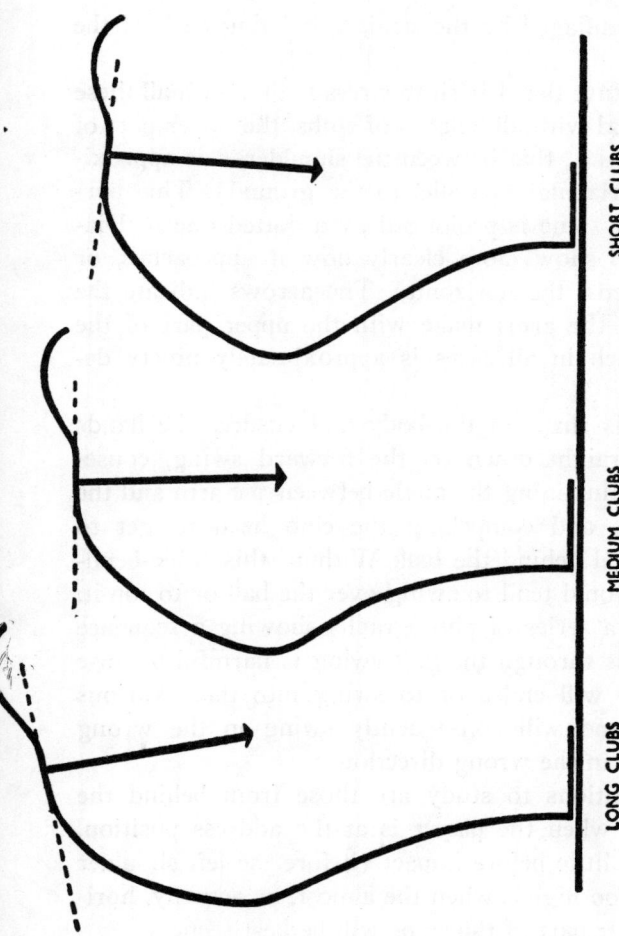

DIAGRAM 4. SILHOUETTES OF EXPERTS

Note (from behind the shot) *first*, the resemblance (with any club) of the body shape to a reversed question mark, this becoming more so with shorter clubs; *second*, the practically horizontal upper part of the spine; and, *third*, the practically perpendicular arms (represented by the arrows). With slight variations of this leg- and back-bending, photographs of most experts conform to this diagram. If you have to stand more upright than this, your clubs are too long. Shorten them.

what camouflaged by the straight-hanging back of the trousers.

The feature that I wish to stress is that with all these players, and with all lengths of clubs, the upper part of the spine—*i.e.,* that between the shoulders—is approximately horizontal (parallel to the ground). This portion of the spine is prolonged by a dotted line in Diagram 4 to show more clearly how it approaches, or even exceeds, the horizontal. The arrows indicate the angle that the arms make with the upper part of the spine, which in all cases is approximately ninety degrees.

It is this shape of the body that ensures the hands coming straight down on the forward swing, consequently maintaining the angle between the arm and the club shaft, and compelling the club head to get to ground level behind the ball. Without this spine-bending, you would tend to swing over the ball or to top it.

I think a series of photographs showing a sequence of positions through the golf swing is harmful because the reader will endeavor to swing into these various positions and will consequently swing in the wrong manner or in the wrong direction.

The positions to study are those from behind the shot: (1) when the player is at the address position, and (2) a little before impact (before the left shoulder has risen too high), when the almost, or actually, horizontal upper part of the spine will be best seen.

The first eight inches or so below the neck, which connects the two shoulders, is the vital part of the spine in golf.

In photographs, as also in the diagram, it will be seen that with all clubs this part of the back, and therefore the spine, is approximately parallel to the ground at the address and just before impact.

Also obvious in experts' photographs is the arm position. At the address and just before impact it is virtually at right angles to the upper part of the spine. Therefore the arms hang down vertically, except maybe with the longer clubs when the hands may be just a little further forward.

Length of Club Shaft

Intimately connected with back-bending is the subject of length of club shaft.

I am certain that many people would play better golf if they shortened their club shafts. Most average golfers play short shots better than long ones. With short clubs they have to bend their backs. Many handicap golfers prefer the mashie to the driver, and often get as far with it. Again, many players cannot use the Number 2. Professionals know that these facts are indisputable.

The difficulty is due to the length of shaft necessitating the player's standing too erect. When I made this discovery, I had my long clubs shortened, with immediate and marked benefit. Theoretically, the club head should travel faster at impact with a longer shaft; in practice, if the club does not fit the player, it does not.

Again, many of the modern short-backswing professionals claim to drive as far with a short backswing as they can with the longer backswing, even though the club head has a shorter journey to impact, just as it has when the club is shorter.

Even if we admit that there might be a slight loss of length, is it not better to have reasonable length down the middle every time than an occasional shot that goes a few yards further?

Before having your shafts shortened, experiment by putting a rubber band on all long shafts, placing the band at the length of your favorite club, and then grip below it. The bit of shaft above your left hand may worry you, but I think the result will surprise you.

If the shortened shafts necessitate an alteration of the "lie," it is a simple matter with the irons. During my many experiments I had my irons acetylene-blow-torched and bent at the neck on two occasions by a local firm. The woods might need new heads. Actually, however, the shaft-shortening will not usually call for alteration of the lie because, if the club head was flat on the ground when you were standing too erect, then when you make the upper part of your spine horizontal, your hands will go down and the toe of the club head will come up; but when you shorten the club shaft the club head will come nearer to you and will again—usually—be flat on the ground.

I am not suggesting that all clubs should be the same length, but even that might be worth considering, since most of the difference in distance, with different clubs, is due to the degree of loft. The slight distance advantage possible by using varying lengths of shaft is more than outweighed by the difficulties this creates, at any rate in the case of high- and medium-handicap players. With longer shafts there is a gradual pushing forward of hands and the body is less bent, with a consequent flattening of the swing.

I think that most readers will now be persuaded to experiment with shorter shafts.

Before leaving this subject of back-bending and clubs to fit the player, I will mention another relevant fact. Observant golfers must have noticed that many professionals have round shoulders. This is because their backs are constantly bent during play, so that ultimately the upper part of their spines becomes permanently nearer the horizontal than the vertical. It could well be termed an occupational deformity, as some of them walk about with the upper part of their bodies in something approaching the address position, or set.

Remember, a crouching attitude is necessary to hit a ball on the ground.

Body Movements

It is necessary to have a clear mental picture of the golf swing, particularly as it affects the player's body. Then, the same body movements can be made every time instead of the mind being full of many possible ways of hitting the ball, each method fighting for supremacy.

The mental picture is of the shoulders revolving

around the upper part of the spine, at right angles to its axis, a quarter of a circle on the backswing and half a circle on the forward swing.

This at once implies the body acting before, and doing more than, the arms.

This mental picture is so important that it will bear amplification so that it will be impressed on the reader's mind, never to be forgotten. I will call it the *First Golden Rule:*

The conscious part of any golf swing, back and forward, is essentially a perpendicular turning of the shoulders around a horizontal upper part of the spine.

That is all you do consciously.

All other movements that occur below the level of the armpits—including those of the hips, legs, and feet—during the course of the golf swing, are secondary, compensatory, subconscious, and occur automatically, without any assistance from the player.

ANGLES OF ADDRESS

I will now clarify Diagram 5, which illustrates angles of address.

In each of the figures of this diagram there are three vertical planes, two right angles, and one obtuse angle.

1. The three vertical planes are the legs, the arms (including the shoulders), and the head. The arms and shoulders are further forward than the legs, and the head is further forward than the arms. Think of these three planes as being relatively parallel.

2. The two right angles are those formed, first, by the arms and the upper part of the spine, and second,

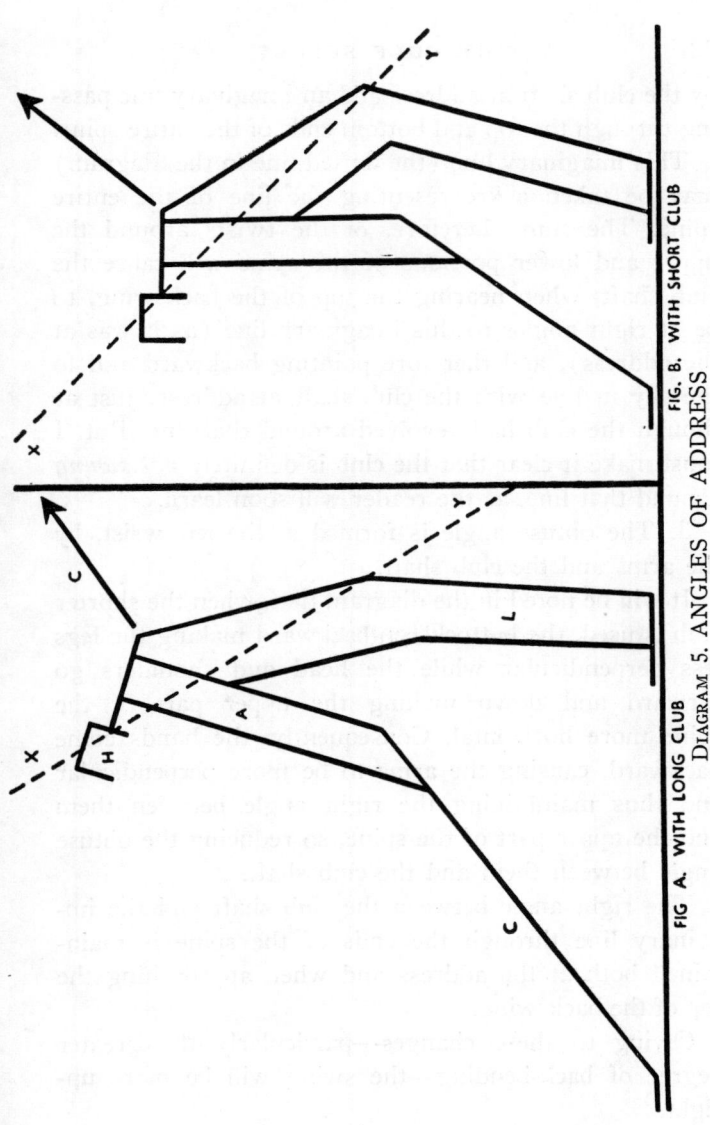

FIG. A. WITH LONG CLUB   FIG. B. WITH SHORT CLUB

DIAGRAM 5. ANGLES OF ADDRESS

The Club XY—The "Entire Spine"

L—The Legs   A—The Arms   H—The Head   C—The Club XY—The "Entire Spine"

by the club shaft at address and an imaginary line passing through the top and bottom ends of the entire spine.

This imaginary line (the dotted line in the diagram) may be taken as representing the line of the entire spine. The sum, therefore, of the twists around the upper and lower portions of the spine will cause the club shaft, when nearing the top of the backswing, to be at right angles to this imaginary line (as it was at the address), and therefore pointing backward and to the sky in line with the club shaft at address, just as though the club had revolved around that line. But, I must make it clear that the club is definitely *not swung* around that line, as the reader will soon learn.

3. The obtuse angle is formed at the left wrist, by the arms and the club shaft.

It will be noted in the diagram that, when the shorter club is used, the buttocks go backward making the legs less perpendicular while the head and shoulders go forward and down making the upper part of the spine more horizontal. Consequently, the hands come backward, causing the arms to be more perpendicular and thus maintaining the right angle between them and the upper part of the spine, so reducing the obtuse angle between them and the club shaft.

The right angle between the club shaft and the imaginary line through the ends of the spine is maintained both at the address and when approaching the top of the backswing.

Owing to these changes—particularly the greater degree of back-bending—the swing will be more upright.

Function of Spine

Before proceeding to a detailed study of the action of the spine in the golf swing, it will be well to have some understanding of the spine's elementary anatomy and function.

The spine consists of a number of separate segments, called vertebrae, which may be likened to a string of large square beads. Imagine the string being pulled very tight. Then, as with the spine, a little movement would be possible in all directions, including a slight twist.

Apart from your ability to bend forward, that twist is the important movement in the golf swing. Now for details.

In the neck there are seven cervical vertebrae. In the chest there are twelve costal vertebrae, so called because the ribs are attached to them. Between the ribs and the hip bones there are five lumbar vertebrae; and below these there is the fixed portion of the spine, the sacrum, by means of which the spine is attached to the pelvis, or hip bones.

Let us see to what extent it is possible to twist the spine.

The cervical spine—*i.e.,* the portion of the spine in the neck—will twist approximately seventy degrees; the remainder, the combined costal and lumbar spine, will twist only about forty-five degrees.

Stand sideways to a mirror, and turn your head to look into it. This will prove that, without moving the shoulders, about seventy degrees is the maximum turn in the neck spine (that is, of the head) in most people.

Now, keep turning your head until your face is square to the mirror and you will find that your shoulder must go back to some extent.

Incidentally, this demonstrates the desirability of, or at least the reason for, turning the head to the right when addressing the ball. It permits a full shoulder pivot of ninety degrees.

Many famous players don't turn their heads to the right at address; instead, they allow their heads to be turned to the right during the course of the backswing by the full shoulder pivot.

With lesser players, who are so determined to keep their heads still that they thereby prevent a full shoulder turn, it is definitely preferable to turn the head at address.

Each person should find out in which of these categories he fits, then adopt the method that suits him.

Personally, I prefer to look straight at the ball in a natural manner and allow the head to be turned, both on the backswing and the forward swing, by the shoulders. While you are swinging, as I will later describe, your head will turn naturally, and you need not worry about head-up.

Now, to continue the study of the spine twist, stand erect, this time facing a mirror, and twist your shoulders ninety degrees to the right into the position they should be in at the top of the backswing. You will find that your hips have turned (automatically and without your help, or even knowledge) approximately half as far as your shoulders—*i.e.,* forty-five degrees.

THE GOLF SECRET—FIRST FACTOR 31

The difference, therefore, between the hip and shoulder turns (forty-five degrees) represents the maximum amount of twist possible in the combined costal and lumbar spines—or, for our purpose, the entire spine.

In many older people the spine will not twist to that extent. Therefore, if they wish to play worth-while golf, they will have to choose between two methods of playing a full shot, both imperfect:

1. A full shoulder pivot with almost as much hip pivot, which will compel the left heel to come too far off the ground.

2. A part shoulder pivot with a normal hip pivot, which will leave the heel down but will shorten the backswing. This will usually be the better method.

Before attempting the impossible on a golf course, see what you are capable of in a mirror. Bearing in mind the shape of the spine as a whole when you are correctly addressing the ball (see Diagrams 4 and 5), we will trace what happens to this spine during the course of the golf swing, briefly indicating what happens to other parts of the body in consequence.

On the backswing the horizontal upper part of the spine is twisted on its axis to the right. This carries the arms, hands, and club straight to the right, while the left shoulder goes down and the right shoulder goes up; and both hips move slightly to the right. Very soon that upper part of the spine is tightly twisted; then the lower, more vertical part of the spine also twists to the right. This carries the shoulders, arms, hands, and club somewhat around you, or "inside the line." The entire spine is now screwed tightly to the right, and that happens soon since a twist of only forty-five degrees is possible.

To continue the backswing, something else must give. The twisted spine pulls the left hip forward and pushes the right hip backward, which carries the shoulders, arms, hands, and club still farther around you. Meanwhile, the left shoulder goes farther down and the right shoulder farther up.

On the forward swing this winding-up is undone progressively, and then there is a winding-up to the left, the process beginning subconsciously in the lower, more vertical part of the spine.

During the first small portion of the voluntary unwinding of the upper part of the spine, there is a greater (though automatic) unwinding of the more vertical lower part of the spine, resulting in a backward movement of the left hip. (This fact, which will be better understood after reading Chapter 2, causes many players, including some experts, to think the forward swing is begun with the left hip.)

As the lower, more vertical part of the spine continues to wind to the left, the winding process is passed upward to the horizontal upper part of the spine, which in turn finally becomes completely wound to the left—after impact. At this stage, since the spine-twisting is complete, the right hip is pulled further forward by the impetus of the swing.

Upright and Flat Swings

It is often said that an open stance (left foot drawn back from line of ball's flight) causes an upright

THE GOLF SECRET—FIRST FACTOR 33

swing. I think not. The left foot, being further back, in effect shortens the left leg, which naturally tends to check the automatic hip turn to the right. If this occurs, it gives the appearance of an upright swing. With the same degree of back-bending the swing can be upright or flat only if the swing itself varies—*i.e.*, if in some instances the swing is wrongly executed. For example, using the hands to hold the face shut on the backswing, or swaying, will tend to produce an exaggerated upright swing; while deliberately opening the club face on the backswing by a wrist roll and/or swinging the club round the right leg will produce a flat swing.

These are wrong methods necessitating different swings for different shots.

A true flat or upright swing depends on the degree of erectness or bending of the body. Providing the swing is always the same (which it should be, unless you prefer to complicate the game), then the more erect the body the flatter the swing will be, and the more bent the body the more upright.

That is why, with a shorter club shaft the swing automatically becomes more upright. And that is why a tall player, who must bend to reach the ball, almost invariably swings upright; while the short player—if he uses clubs of average length, which will be too long for him—must stand more erect and usually swings flat.

The Feel of the Golf Swing

I am going to describe what I believe to be a unique method of acquiring the feel of the golf swing.

Grip a golf club, then stand perfectly upright with arms reasonably outstretched in front of you. Your hands should be about level with the middle of your stomach, your shoulders should be forward, and your upper arms lightly touching your chest. The club shaft will be horizontal—*i.e.,* parallel to the floor.

Now swing the club straight around to the right, then straight around to the left, so that you feel that your hands and the club are traveling in a "straight line" (by which I mean all the time on the same plane, parallel to the floor).

Repeat several times until you get some freedom; then swing to the right, stop, and look. Actually, the hands have gone a little higher than you felt; also, the left hand is higher than the right because it is tending to turn over the right one. Notice that you did not consciously perform that "turn of the wrists," as it is called. You must not. It happens automatically. You will also see the left arm straight and the right arm bent at the elbow, which is down. You did not consciously do that. You must not. It happens automatically.

Where is the club? The shaft is pointing rather backward, and the face of the club is facing part way to the sky. You did not voluntarily put it into that position. Once more, you must not. It goes there automatically.

During a "live" swing, the hands beyond this point rise a little higher still, lifting the right elbow off the body; and the impetus of the swing carries the club head further back until it swings toward your back to point at the target—*i.e.,* to your left.

The momentum of the swing in this final stage completes the gradual cocking of your wrists. You did not consciously do that. You must not.

Remember that all these things have happened, but you felt that you had merely swung your arms around to the right, flat, in a straight line, parallel to the floor, thus revolving your spine.

Now, swing in the same flat arc to the left, and you will observe to all intents and purposes the same phenomena: your hands have crossed and gone up, the right arm is straight while the left one is bent. You did not do these things voluntarily. Nor must you.

Actually, there are slight differences when swinging to the left, all due to the fact that the left hand is higher on the club shaft.

Didn't you feel great power in that swing? But you did not feel very secure on your legs.

You have now executed the correct orthodox golf swing with the part of your body above the armpits, except that the swing should have been on an almost perpendicular plane, instead of, as it was, horizontal.

It will be noticed that in the upper part of the swing —*i.e.,* of shoulders, arms, and club—there are many automatic occurrences; but in the lower part—*i.e.,* of hips, legs, and feet—*every* movement is automatic.

It was the lower part of the swing that made you insecure on your feet because it was entirely rotatory, which it should not be.

When the back is bent, making the upper part of the spine almost horizontal, then the upper, conscious part of the backswing is to the right and upward; the lower, subconscious part of the swing moves in the same general direction before it is automatically forced into a partly rotatory movement. This subtle difference produces a check to the end of the backswing and a consequent feeling of perfect balance.

The same rule applies to the forward swing. The upper, conscious part is to the left and upward, and the lower, subconscious part moves in the same direction before turning to the left, thus ensuring good balance.

It can be accepted that, if you set any part of your body in motion in a certain direction, the first movement of the remainder of your body will be in the same direction.

Prove this by swinging an arm around you, and observe your whole body twist in the same direction. Then swing an arm straight to one side and upward, and your body will move in the same direction. You made only one purposeful movement; all the other movements were subconscious and compensatory—*i.e.,* for the purpose of maintaining your balance. So it is with golf. The entire swing is performed by the upper part of your body, that part of your body to which your arms are attached. Grasp that fact.

The Correct Attitude

We will now briefly deal with the swing in the correct golfing attitude.

THE GOLF SECRET—FIRST FACTOR 37

Stand upright, gripping a golf club that is parallel to the floor. For the next step, don't move your shoulder joints so as to move your hands nearer to, or further from, your body; and don't alter the shape of your wrists, thereby altering the angle between your arms and the club shaft. Merely bend your back, particularly the upper part (see Diagram 5), until the club head rests on the ground. You will then be in the correct and natural position for hitting a golf ball that is on the ground as described at the beginning of this chapter.

A good way of assuming this position and getting used to it is to let the arms hang in front of the legs and clear of them, and then to look intently at a spot on the ground about two feet in front of you as though you were looking for a half dollar—as if you wanted to get your eyes nearer the ground! You will be surprised how big a golf ball looks when you look at it in this way.

Having struck the correct attitude, everything is plain sailing. The backswing and the forward swing are performed in exactly the same manner as when you were standing erect, by revolving your shoulders around the upper part of your spine.

All the things that happened automatically when you stood erect will occur automatically now, the only differences being that the swing will feel to be vertical and in a straight line instead of horizontal and rotatory, and that there is a check to the end of the backswing and the forward swing, in consequence of which you will feel secure on your feet.

The first factor of the Golf Secret is that the upper part of the spine must be horizontal or nearly so, thus permitting a practically perpendicular revolving of the shoulders around it to execute both the backswing and the forward swing, every movement in all parts of the body below this level—*i.e.*, of hips, legs, and feet—being entirely subconscious, compensatory, and automatic.

Chapter 2

THE GOLF SECRET—SECOND FACTOR

The Left Shoulder
The Golf Swing Wheel
Backswing—
  First Movement
  Direction of Left-shoulder Movement
  Expert Confirmation
  Experts' Contradictory Beliefs
  Effects of Correct Left-shoulder Movement
Forward Swing—
  First Movement
  Direction of Left-shoulder Movement
  Speed of Shoulder Movement
  Likely Misgivings
  Expert Confirmation
  Experts' Contradictory Beliefs
  Effects of Correct Left-shoulder Movement
  Convince Yourself
Limber-up

THE LEFT SHOULDER

I consider the left shoulder to be the most important part of the anatomy used in the golf swing. If you think **only** of the left shoulder to the exclusion of everything else, you will play better golf than if you don't think of it, no matter what else you do.

I am convinced that the left shoulder alone consciously begins the backswing and also begins the forward swing, and contributes much of the force and power to it.

Before attempting to prove my contentions, it is necessary that the reader should have a very definite idea of what I mean by "left shoulder," since it could mean any one of three things.

1. I do not mean the shoulder joint, which is formed by the shoulder blade (the scapula) and the top end of the upper arm bone (the humerus). This joint is used when you wish to move the upper arm.

It is important to realize that, without using the joint, its position in relation to the chest can be varied in three different ways:

a. Upward, as when you shrug your shoulders.

b. Backward, as when you brace your shoulders to produce a soldierly appearance.

c. Forward, as when you bring your shoulders forward and consequently nearer together, making yourself flat-chested. Incidentally, this is the position into which you should put your shoulders when addressing a golf ball.

2. I do not mean the shoulder muscles that cover the shoulder joint and bring it into action when you wish to move the upper arm.

3. I mean the "architectural" shoulder, which might be called the top left corner of the body.

During the course of the golf swing, the shoulder-joint position in relation to the chest is not altered, except involuntarily near the end of the backswing and again near the end of the forward swing: therefore, for our purpose I would like the reader to regard it as being fixed to, and part of, the chest.

A downward or upward movement of the shoulder

(as defined) is a very complicated body movement, but there is no point in describing the many muscles involved because the movement is quite easily performed without the knowledge. The important thing is that the left shoulder is the point of concentration, and its movement can be easily visualized.

The Golf Swing Wheel

Now study Diagram 6, which represents a golfer ready to begin the backswing and the path his club head would take. Note the resemblance to a wheel. (For the sake of clarity the right arm is not depicted.)

To start any wheel in motion the force is applied to the hub, then transmitted centrifugally through the spokes to the rim.

Since it is acknowledged by all that the spine (some say neck or head, which are extensions of the spine) is the hub of the golf swing, it is obvious that we must find the best method of making that hub revolve on its axis, to begin and complete the backswing and the forward swing. To enable the club head to return to the ball on the forward swing, it is desirable to prevent the hub from changing its position (either upward, downward, forward, backward, or to right or left) in relation to the ball.

Backswing—First Movement

Since probably every authority with one exception agrees that the backswing is not begun with any part of the right side of the body, we can accept that.

For the moment I am leaving out of account such

stunts as the forward press, which in any case should be regarded as an involuntary movement.

By reference to Diagram 6 it will be seen that it is possible to set the hub revolving to the right by moving any one of four portions of the total left arm—the hand, the forearm, the upper arm, or the shoulder. Let us consider what is likely to happen when you begin the backswing by these various agencies.

1. *The Hand.* If you pick up any small article from a table, you will see that your wrist will bend backward as you do so. The same thing happens when you begin the backswing with your left hand: the wrist at once begins to "break" or "roll." Therefore the hands should not be used to start the backswing, because this early wrist-cocking is then bound to occur—and even the experts are agreed that this is wrong!

It should now be obvious that so-called "hands-first" to start the backswing—*i.e.,* hands before club head—cannot be achieved by concentrating on the hands. Hands-first occurs naturally and automatically when the left shoulder is pushed down, which causes the arm, then the hands, and finally the club head to move to the right.

2. *The Forearm.* Similarly, using the forearm would tend at once to bend the elbow. This is also natural and to be expected but very undesirable so early in the backswing, for there can be no semblance of a straight left arm and the swing would be anything but wide.

3. *The Upper Arm.* To begin the backswing with the left upper arm (which would be done by the shoul-

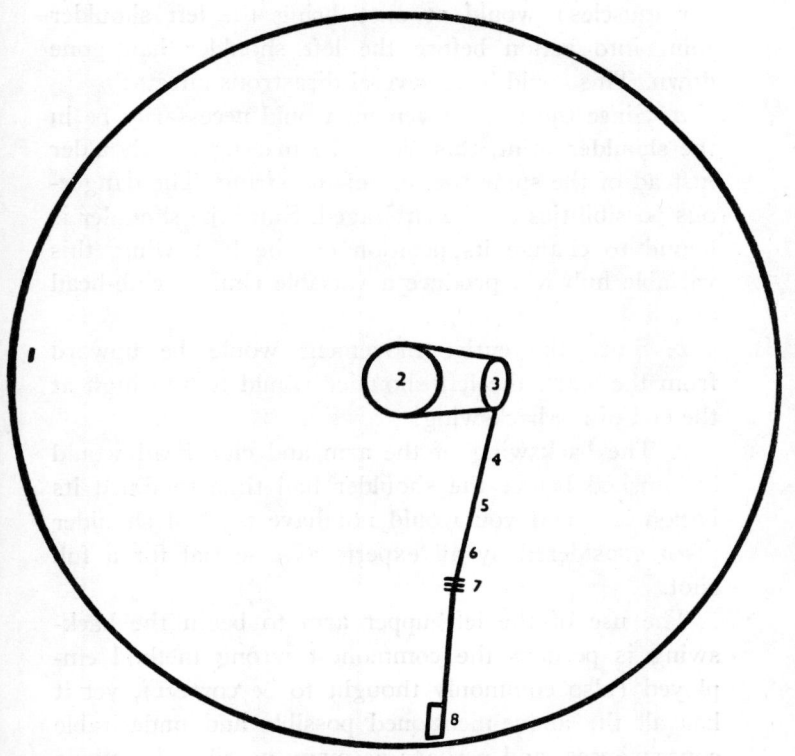

DIAGRAM 6. THE GOLF SWING WHEEL

1—RIM OF WHEEL, OR PATH OF CLUB HEAD
2—HUB OF WHEEL, OR HUB OF THE SWING—*i.e.*, UPPER SPINE
3—LEFT SHOULDER
4—UPPER ARM
5—ELBOW
6—FOREARM
7—HAND, GRIPPING CLUB
8—CLUB HEAD
2 to 8—SPOKE OF WHEEL

der muscles) would at once bring the left shoulder joint into action before the left shoulder had gone down. This could have several disastrous effects:

a. Since the first movement would necessarily be in the shoulder joint, this would be making the shoulder instead of the spine the hub of the swing. The dangerous possibilities can be envisaged. Since the shoulder is bound to change its position on the backswing, this variable hub will produce a variable rim, or club-head arc.

b. Since the entire movement would be upward from the start, the left shoulder would be too high at the end of the backswing.

c. The backswing of the arm and club head would be finished before the shoulder had time to finish its backswing, and you would not have the full shoulder pivot considered by all experts as essential for a full shot.

The use of the left upper arm to begin the backswing is perhaps the commonest wrong method employed (also commonly thought to be correct), yet it has all the above-mentioned possible and undesirable consequences, and perhaps as many possible directions for the ball to travel, owing to incomplete shoulder turn and the left shoulder's being too high. A frequent result would be contacting of the ball from outside the line, thus producing a slice.

There is one fault common to all three of the above-mentioned methods of starting the backswing. None of them sets the swing wheel in motion by first causing the hub to revolve. Instead, they first move the joint

THE GOLF SECRET—SECOND FACTOR

immediately above the part used—*i.e.,* the hand moves the wrist, the forearm moves the elbow, and the upper arm moves the shoulder joint.

4. *The Shoulder.* For our purpose the shoulder is a fixed point, firmly attached through the chest to the upper part of the spine; therefore, any movement of the shoulder (not the joint) will at once cause the hub to revolve. The left shoulder is the part to think of when we wish to begin the backswing. The advantages of this method will be more fully appreciated when we come to consider the sequence of events that accompanies it, but before doing that we must decide the exact direction in which we intend to move the left shoulder.

BACKSWING—DIRECTION OF LEFT-SHOULDER MOVEMENT

We can begin this investigation by asking a question. What happens to the left shoulder during the course of the golf swing? The answer is: all sorts of things with the average golfer, but with first-class players the left shoulder moves always in the same direction, and that is why they get a grooved swing with every shot.

Since we have shown that the upper part of the spine is horizontal, or nearly so, it must be obvious that to revolve it the first movement of the left shoulder must be downward, perpendicularly or nearly so; and since on the backswing the left shoulder should finish in front of the neck, pointing over the ball, it is apparent that it must travel through a quarter of a circle downward and to the right. Naturally, when the left shoulder is in front of the neck, the right shoulder is behind. In other words, the shoulders have been twisted around the upper part of the spine.

I assure you it is possible to go wrong on this apparently simple movement. If you think too much of the shoulder going to the right, you are apt to turn it to the right too soon—*i.e.,* before it has gone far enough down. This would restrict the shoulder turn and leave the left shoulder too high at the end of the backswing.

In actual practice it will usually be found better to think only of left shoulder down; then, when it has gone down as far as it can, it is bound to turn to the right if you keep the hub (the upper spine) in the same position. At the same time visualize that quarter circle.

The more nearly horizontal the upper spine is (say with a short club), then the more perpendicularly will the left shoulder go down. Geometrically, this should put the right shoulder perpendicularly above the left one, which, of course, it does not. Those who have learned the previous chapter will know that this is because, after the upper part of the spine has tightened to the right, then the lower, more perpendicular part of the spine also tightens to the right, and in so doing it *turns* both shoulders; therefore the right one goes backward and the left one forward. It is lack of the knowledge of this twofold action of the spine that is responsible for so much confused thought and teaching. Because the left shoulder finishes in a forward position, it is presumed that it has been consciously turned into that position. Do thoroughly understand this principle because, if the backswing starts right, it is likely to finish right; and, further, if the backswing is right, the forward swing will probably be right.

It will now be apparent that the magic quarter circle is on an inclined plane downward, forward, and to the right. But remember that you merely push the left shoulder down and that its apparent forward turn is due to the automatic hip turn. We can now formulate our *Second Golden Rule:*

Begin and complete the backswing by pushing the left shoulder down.

Whether or not the reader is convinced that the backswing should be begun with the left shoulder, he will agree that it must traverse the path that I have outlined. When he admits that, he must also admit that the most certain way to make it do so is to push it down.

A full shoulder pivot is the most important requirement for any full shot, and failure in this respect is the most common error. Concentration on the left shoulder will make a full shoulder pivot inevitable.

Backswing—Expert Confirmation

No matter what you may hear to the contrary, it is a fact that at the top of the backswing in the case of most of the world's leading players, the left shoulder is quite low down even when using the driver. Photographs in most pictorial golf books show the shoulder line to form an angle with the perpendicular, of approximately forty-five degrees.

It will be recalled that the left-shoulder joint is subconsciously lifted to a higher level by the upswinging arm toward the end of the backswing. Prove this, by feeling with your right hand, the outer end of your left collarbone rise as you push your left arm upward. But the left side of the chest does not rise. If you bear these two facts in mind when studying the above-mentioned shoulder line at the top of the backswing, you will realize that the top left-hand corner of the body is actually even further down than it appears to be.

Backswing—Experts' Contradictory Beliefs

It is a fact that twelve golf experts—including many of today's leading players—have written books in which they each describe the commencement of the backswing differently. That is to say, no two descriptions are alike. Obviously at least eleven of them must be wrong! Only three of the twelve mention the left shoulder at all (they are on the right track), but since all their left shoulders must, and do, go down, it is just possible that they all begin the backswing with the left shoulder without being aware of it.

Some of these writers make the game even more complicated by describing different methods of starting the backswing with different clubs.

Don't take my word for the above statement. Compare the descriptions in the books you possess.

Don't make the game more difficult than it is: simplify it. Begin all shots with a downward movement of the left shoulder.

Backswing—Effects of Correct Left-shoulder Movement

We must now study Diagram 7 and consider the sequence of events that stems from the downward movement of the left shoulder.

No. 9 (in Diagram 7) represents the abruptly curved arc that results from incorrectly starting the backswing with hand or forearm.

The different positions of the component parts in Figures *A* and *B* represent what happens during the early part of the backswing, when the shoulders correctly revolve around the horizontal upper part of the spine.

It should be clearly understood that, whereas in an earlier section I described what a golfer should consciously do to start the backswing, I am now going to describe what subconsciously happens to the arms and the club in consequence.

As the left shoulder starts to go downward, the force is passed centrifugally through the "spoke" to the "rim" of the wheel, so that the club head is the last to move. As the left shoulder goes down, the right shoulder goes up the same distance. This carries the hands straight back to the right on the same level; therefore, the club head also goes straight back on the same level—*i.e.,* close to the ground as it should—and, consequently, the arc is flattened and a wide swing is ensured. I do not mean to give the impression that this sequence of events will make a straight left arm a certainty, but there will be less tendency for the arm to

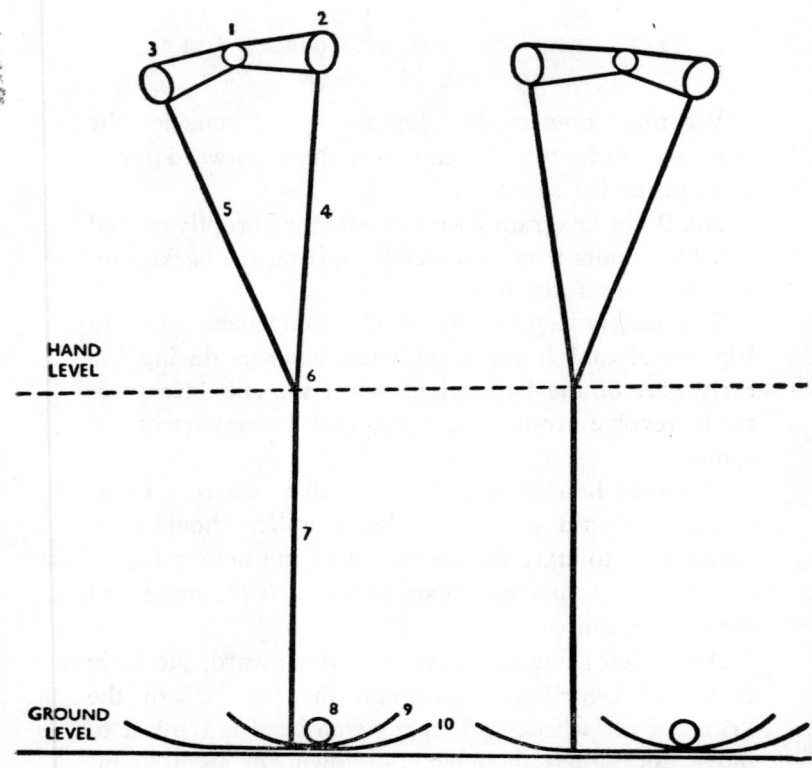

FIG. A. ADDRESS FIG B. BACKSWING BEGUN

Diagram 7. THE FLATTENED ARC

1—Horizontal Upper Spine
2—Left Shoulder
3—Right Shoulder
4—Left Arm
5—Right Arm
6—Hands
7—Club
8—Ball
9—Curved Arc
10—Flattened Arc

bend; there will, therefore, be less difficulty in keeping it straight. That will tend further to widen the swing.

If you made the mistake of consciously pushing the club head back to the right close to the ground with your hand or arm, you would tend to sway, or even to look at the club head as it went back. Think only of your left shoulder, and the club head will automatically traverse its correct course.

When your left shoulder is halfway down, your hands and the club are about waist high. That is, the backswing is half completed without any conscious help from your arms. The part played by your arms, activated by the shoulder muscles, will be revealed in the next chapter.

A more complete description of the automatic occurrences will be given in the final chapter.

Forward Swing—First Movement

As was shown in the previous chapter, the forward swing is begun simply by revolving the shoulders around the horizontal upper part of the spine. The same rule applies (and for similar reasons) as in the backswing. That is, set the hub revolving by the nearest part of the left side of your anatomy to it—*i.e.,* the left shoulder. A strong argument in favor of beginning the forward swing with the left shoulder is that, as you performed the backswing with it, why transfer your concentration to another part of the body? In the split second necessary to execute the golf swing, you have not time to think of different things, either together or in sequence; therefore, think only of the most vital—the left shoulder.

Forward Swing—Direction of Left-shoulder Movement

On the backswing the left shoulder traversed a quarter of a circle downward and to the right. On the forward swing it retraces its steps on that quarter circle (hence, the grooved swing) and continues the almost vertical circular motion until it is behind the neck, at which stage the right shoulder is under the chin. The head then turns left, and the whole body (both shoulders and head) moves to the left as the shot finishes.

The left shoulder, then, travels at least a half circle. Get this magic half circle well fixed in your mind and visualize it on every shot: left shoulder to the left, upward, then to the right.

You have often heard of getting the left hip out of the way, but as we have demonstrated, it gets out of the way automatically. You have not heard of getting the left shoulder out of the way, which is very important for the following reason: Because the left hand is higher than the right one on the club shaft, then in effect the left arm is three inches longer than the right arm. This additional length of left arm will block the blow of the forward swing (resulting in a curtailed swing or follow-through, or a bent left arm at impact) unless the left shoulder is got out of the way. It is the half-circle movement that gets the left shoulder out of the way. Get this point clear: as the hands and the club are going "through the ball" followed by the right shoulder, the left shoulder is moving in the opposite direction—to the right, away from the shot. It is probable that the last part of this half circle should be the fastest part, since it coincides with impact, or soon after, which is when the club head should be traveling fastest.

Just as you could go wrong on the backswing quarter circle, so you can go wrong on the forward-swing half circle. If you should mistakenly concentrate on the movement to the left or right of the half circle, you will, respectively, carry too much weight to the left or keep it to the right. On the other hand, if you concentrate on the upward part of the half circle, provided you keep the hub in the same place and visualize the half circle, then the shoulder must move to the left first and must move to the right after it goes up.

It amounts to this: since on the backswing the downward element in the movement of the left shoulder was the important part, so on the forward swing you must concentrate on its opposite—the upward part—to obtain a grooved swing.

This all seems so obvious that I almost blush to make such a fuss about it, but I know how vitally important it is; and yet I have never heard or read anything about it. You need only try what I have suggested to convince yourself of its truth.

It is important to realize that the inclined plane of the forward-swing half circle (like that of the backswing quarter circle) is an illusion and is due to the automatic turn of the hips, whereas the conscious plane of the shoulder movement is perpendicular because the upper part of the spine is horizontal.

Forward Swing—Speed of Shoulder Movement

After a momentary pause of the left shoulder in front of your neck at the top of the backswing, you should start, and complete, the forward swing as quickly as possible by pulling your left shoulder up quickly. Don't think of beginning the forward swing slowly and gradually increasing the pace. You have no option but to begin slowly since you are reversing the direction, but since the forward swing is all over in a split second, you must think of speed from the start. The more quickly you take your left shoulder up, the more quickly the club head will come down and through the ball and the further the ball will go. That quick shoulder movement is the quick turn of the shoulders that has been described as occurring in all professionals. My repeated use of the word "quick" is to impress its importance. Quick shoulder movement gives quick swing!

Forward Swing—Likely Misgivings

1. You may imagine that, since at the top of the backswing your left shoulder is pointing over the ball, to pull it upward would push the club out to the right in an exaggerated inside-to-out swing. Actually, it is this movement that produces the much vaunted inside-to-out swing—it ensures the club head staying "inside the

line" until near impact. But there is another factor that prevents the inside-to-out swing from being exaggerated. Just as on the backswing all that you felt you did was to swing on a straight line upward to the right (the swing being carried around subconsciously by the automatic hip turn), so on the forward swing all you feel you do is to reverse the direction by swinging on a straight line upward to the left—the automatic hip turn bringing your shoulders square to the ball at impact.

Every golf shot is a straight-line shot!

2. Don't let anyone tell you that swinging upward will make you top the ball. Diagram 7 shows how the coincident up-and-down movements of the right and left shoulders, together with the hands traveling onward, flatten the arc of the swing at the bottom. This will prevent any rising of the club head before it should happen and will therefore prevent topping.

3. Thinking of performing the forward swing quickly from the start will not make you "snatch" because you are not thinking of hands or club; they will take care of themselves, and, in fact, will still be going backward as your left shoulder starts to go forward.

Forward Swing—Expert Confirmation

Let us examine Diagram 8 and note what is common to most experts. In it will be seen the approximate shoulder line of most professionals at, or soon after, impact. This is a composite diagram based on photographs in pictorial golf books of twenty-five expert golfers, mostly British and American professionals. There are, of course, variations of a few degrees either way with different players.

Figure *A* (viewed from in front of the player) shows the angle formed by a line through the shoulders to be about forty-five degrees to the perpendicular.

Figure *B* (viewed from the right of the player) shows the angle formed by a line through the shoulders to be only about twenty degrees to the perpendicular.

Both figures prove that the left shoulder is considerably higher at, and after, impact than at address, and also that it is definitely going upward and not turning to the left.

Forward Swing—Experts' Contradictory Beliefs

As we found with the backswing, twelve experts —including many present-day leading players—have written describing the beginning of the forward swing. Again, all differently! Therefore, at most, only one of them can be right. Two of these experts say, begin by transferring the weight; but neither explains how to do this. We have proved that pulling the left shoulder upward causes automatic weight transference; and since we know that experts' left shoulders do go up, it seems likely that they all start the forward swing that way. As they have been unable to analyze the movement with any semblance of unanimity (compare their books), it is well that someone should do it for them.

Don't complicate the game: simplify it. Always be-

A—SHOULDER LINE SOON AFTER IMPACT (OBSERVER FACING THE PLAYER). SHOULDERS 45 DEGREES TO PERPENDICULAR

    1—LEFT SHOULDER
    2—RIGHT SHOULDER

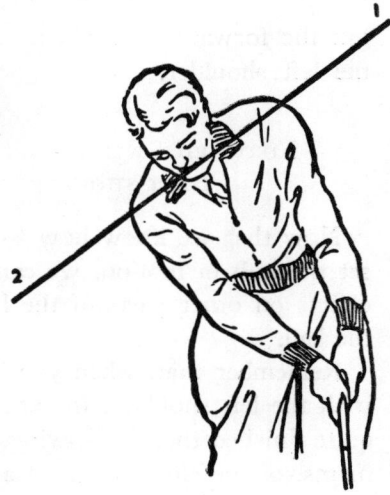

B—SHOULDER LINE SOON AFTER IMPACT (OBSERVER TO RIGHT OF PLAYER, BEHIND THE SHOT). SHOULDERS 30 DEGREES OR LESS TO PERPENDICULAR

    1—LEFT SHOULDER
    2—RIGHT SHOULDER

DIAGRAM 8. THE SHOULDER ANGLES

gin the forward swing with an upward movement of the left shoulder.

Forward Swing—Effects of Correct Left-shoulder Movement

Now that we know how to use the left shoulder to set the hub in motion, we can consider the automatic effects on other parts of the body, the club head, and the ball.

Remember that, when you begin the forward swing with the left shoulder, the arms and the club have not quite finished their backswing. These coincident movements, of the club backward and the left shoulder forward, keep the upper part of the spine wound to the right. This fact (as the left shoulder starts to move) causes the left hip to move to the left and backward (weight transference). This very obvious hip movement is the cause of the erroneous belief that the left hip begins the forward swing.

As the left hip goes backward, the right hip, of course, comes forward, the combined movements constituting the unwinding and rewinding to the left of the lower, more vertical part of the spine. This unwinding and rewinding process is passed upward to the upper, more horizontal part of the spine, thus allowing the left shoulder to accelerate its upward movement, which, in turn, hastens the descent of the arms toward the hitting area, with the wrists still cocked and the club shaft still bent. At the same time, the backward-moving left hip has turned the shoulders to be square

THE GOLF SECRET—SECOND FACTOR

to the ball and has also pushed the left heel on to the ground with a tendency for the foot to roll on to its outside edge. The left foot now becomes the fulcrum of the forward swing.

At this stage the effects of centrifugal force become apparent and cause the rim of the swing wheel to travel faster than the hub. Consequently, the hands and the club pass the body, wrist-cocking (and elbow-cocking, if present) having become automatically undone, so that the club head makes solid contact with the ball, which moves off in a straight line at right angles to the loft of the club face.

As the left shoulder continues its half circle, the hands and the club head go straight forward on the flattened arc until they finally go upward into a high finish, the delayed crossing of the right hand over the left taking place on the way. During this final phase, as the right shoulder passed under the chin, the head turned to the left; then the whole upper part of the body moved to the left, to be supported by a firm left leg; the right leg having been dragged, the right foot rolled on to its inside edge before coming up more or less on its toe.

Note well that the only conscious action was to pull up the left shoulder. All the foot, leg, and hip movements were automatic and secondary to the effort made with the upper part of the body, as was the downward movement of the arms. The wrist uncocking and subsequent hand-crossing were also automatic and due to centrifugal force. The hands did nothing except grip the club shaft.

Forward Swing—Convince Yourself

I will now ask the reader to prove to himself that pulling the left shoulder upward does in fact cause the rest of the body to do what I have said.

Stand absolutely erect; then forcibly raise the left shoulder (by which, again, I mean the "left corner of the body," not the shoulder joint). What happened without your assistance? The left hip moved straight to the left and upward making the left leg firm, and the weight transferred to the left. Lower the shoulder, and the hip and the weight will return to the original position.

Now bend your back until the upper part of your spine is about horizontal, as we have learned it should be when playing golf. Again, forcibly raise the left shoulder. What happened then without your assistance? The weight transferred to the left, and your left hip moved to the left, upward, and backward out of the way, again making the left leg firm. Also, the right hip and knee came forward a little, and the right foot rolled on to its inside edge with a tendency for the heel to rise.

This is proof that, when you play golf, the back should be bent, the forward swing should be started by pulling the left shoulder upward, and that the entire hip, leg, and foot portion of the swing is automatic and secondary to the upward pull of the left shoulder.

Remember the twofold action of the spine! As in the backswing, it is want of this knowledge that accounts for all the confusion in explaining the beginning of the forward swing.

The reader may now convince himself that the forward swing should not only be commenced, but completed, mainly by concentrating on the left shoulder.

Stand erect, gripping a golf club, which will be parallel to the floor when held in front of you, as you did when acquiring the feel of the golf swing. Now swing as you should when hitting a golf ball, fairly slowly to the right and as quickly as you can to the left, feeling all the time that the club shaft remains parallel to the floor.

First of all, try to detect which part of your body appears to start the swing to the left—*i.e.,* the forward swing. I will be surprised if you don't agree that it is your left shoulder or, at least, the left side of your body. If you are doubtful, repeat the swing, but definitely begin and finish the forward swing with your right arm. I think you will find that the blow is weaker, the swing less wide, with less follow-through, and with a tendency for you to remain on your right leg.

Again repeat the swing, this time concentrating on the left shoulder. You will have a feeling of tremendous power, your weight will transfer well to the left, the swing will be wide, and the follow-through complete.

Finally, repeat the swing in the same manner, but after having bent your back until the club head rests on the ground in the way previously described. This time the swing will be upright, and as a result your balance will be better and you will more definitely recognize that you are leading the swing with your left shoulder, not some other part of the left side of your body.

LIMBER-UP

Before leaving the subject of left-shoulder action, a word on limbering-up will not be amiss. We have all seen players swinging reasonably well at daisies on the first tee and then playing dud shots. They would get better results if, instead of merely swinging the club, they would limber-up the shoulders while firmly gripping the club. Get that full, free movement of the left shoulder, alternately in front of and behind the neck.

The second factor of the Golf Secret is that the left shoulder is the point of concentration in revolving the shoulders around the horizontal upper part of the spine in both the backswing and the forward swing, the movement being downward on the backswing and upward on the forward swing, all movement below the chest being secondary to this and automatic.

Chapter 3

THE GOLF SECRET—THIRD FACTOR

> *Voluntary Use of Arms*
> *Choice of Method*
> *Direction of Arm Swing*
> *Expert Confirmation*
> *How to Do It*
> *Short Shots*

In the two preceding chapters I think I have proved that the body plays the major part in the golf swing and provides most of its power.

All leg movements—in fact, all movements below the chest—we are satisfied, are automatic.

It now remains to consider the action of the upper limbs in the golf swing, during which investigation several facts must be kept constantly in mind:

1. Because the upper part of the spine, which is the hub of the swing, is practically horizontal, the swing feels as if it were in a straight line—*i.e.*, straight up to the right, then straight up to the left.

2. The swing appears to go to some extent around the body owing to the subconscious turning of the hips, which carries the shoulders around.

3. On both the backswing and the forward swing the bottom of the arc is flattened by the simultaneous up-and-down movement of the right and left shoulders.

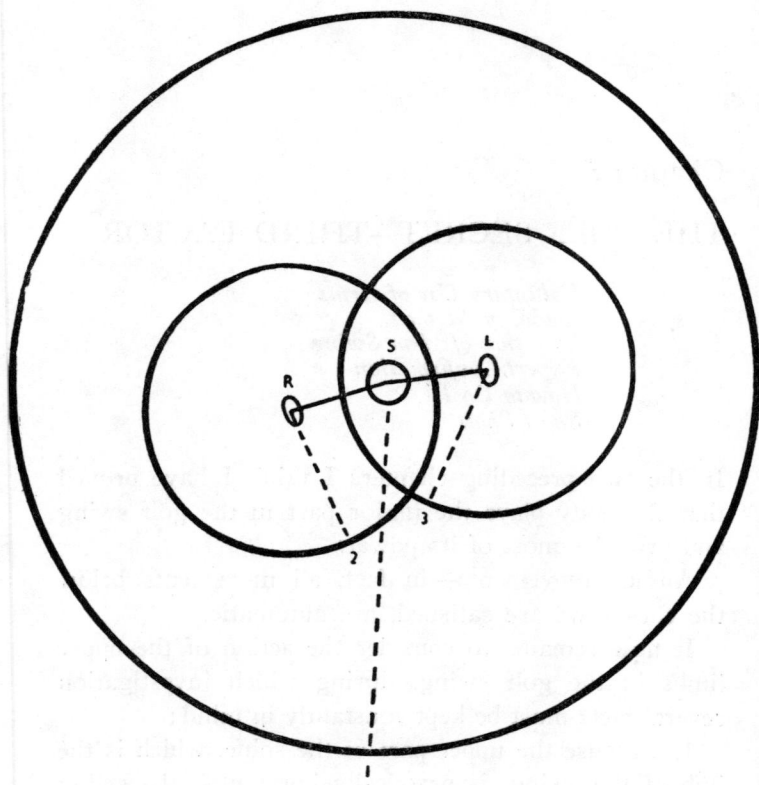

DIAGRAM 9. THE THREE HUBS AND THE THREE ARCS

S—SPINE
R—RIGHT SHOULDER
L—LEFT SHOULDER

1—SPINE ARC
2—RIGHT-SHOULDER ARC
3—LEFT-SHOULDER ARC

The right-shoulder joint is the axis of the right-arm swing, and the left-shoulder joint is the axis of the left-arm swing; but the spine is the central axis of the main, or body, swing. Thus, both shoulders—*i.e.*, the body—and the arms, hands, and the club "attached" to them are merely revolved around the horizontal upper part of the spine. The arm swings may be assisted voluntarily, but centrifugal force is the main factor in synchronizing the three swings, with consequent good timing.

THE GOLF SECRET—THIRD FACTOR

4. The only conscious feeling, apart from the down-and-up left-shoulder movements, is of swinging upward on the backswing and upward on the forward swing.

I have said *ad nauseam* that the upper part of the spine is the hub of the golf swing. But inside that swing there are two other subsidiary hubs and swings. These two hubs are the two shoulder joints, and the two swings are of the arms (see Diagram 9).

It will be realized that, while the spine is the fixed hub, the shoulder joints are movable hubs; and, therefore, while the golf swing is in progress, the arm swings and arcs, together with their hubs, are being revolved in their entirety around the fixed main hub. One might say there are two swings within a swing!

It is, of course, possible to play good golf without any conscious use of the arms, in which case one factor is that the body movement carries the arms part of the way up both on the backswing and the forward swing. Prove that now. You will find that the hands move from one side to the other through at least a half circle.

A second factor in the subconscious use of the arms is centrifugal force and momentum, which carry the arms a little higher.

A third factor is that with the intention to swing the club upward by the body, the shoulder muscles that swing the arms through the shoulder joints will automatically come to your assistance, thus sending the hands still higher.

Voluntary Use of Arms

Of course, it is possible to reinforce the swing by actively swinging the arms with the shoulder muscles, thereby gaining extra length. Long hitters undoubtedly do this. This active use of the shoulder muscles, which is often mistakenly thought to be use of the hands, introduces a stumbling block to the acquisition of a well-timed swing. For good timing and a consequent good shot the three swings must be synchronized. That is to say, the arms must be swung at the correct time in relation to the main swing around the spine.

How can we best achieve this object? It will necessitate first of all deciding with which part of the total arm we are going to swing. It should be obvious that, since we are going to swing the whole arm, we must first move the top end.

Just as, in the case of the spine, we set the main hub in motion by the nearest part to it—*i.e.,* the left shoulder—so here we must set this lesser hub, the shoulder joint, in motion by the nearest part to it—*i.e.,* the upper arm—by means of the shoulder muscles.

However, for the benefit of the cynics and the diehards who still think they swing with their hands, we will take a look at other possibilities. These people probably think that we eat, pick up a tumbler, box, fence, or play tennis or golf with our hands. They are just about as wide of the mark as possible. The hand is used merely to hold, or grip, the implement.

Go through any of these movements now and see if

THE GOLF SECRET—THIRD FACTOR 67

you can detect your hand doing anything but holding on.

Even a table is not thumped with the hand! The hand is merely the end of the arm that makes contact. You could pat it with your hand, which is what you do to a golf ball if you hit with your hands.

The chief muscles used for performing the above—especially when any effort is required, as in playing golf—are those about the shoulders, which raise the upper arms. If anyone doubts that assertion, let him attempt to do any of those things while his upper arms are fixed to his chest by a rope, thus preventing his shoulder muscles from functioning.

It should be recalled that, when we use any part of the arm, it causes a natural movement of the joint immediately above it; then, if necessary for further effort, movement of the joint above that. For example, if you swing back a golf club with your left *hand,* you will find that the wrist begins to bend first, then the elbow, and finally the shoulder joint. These things tend to occur with either hand or with both together, whether on the backswing or the forward swing, with consequent narrowing of the swing. On the forward swing they cause too active wrist work, with too early crossing of the right hand over the left and a consequent likelihood of pulling the ball to the left. See Diagram 10, which serves to demonstrate these points. In practice the wrist and elbow swings are a little wider than indicated owing to partial use of other joints.

I think everyone will now be convinced that the arms must be swung from the shoulder joints by the shoulder muscles acting on the upper arms. By this means we will maintain the wide swing that we have initiated with the left shoulder.

Choice of Method

Compare the two methods of using the arms, both on the backswing and the forward swing. If we allow the arms to function involuntarily and automatically, we will probably lose a little length! But the great problem of timing will be solved. This timing is much more accurate if not interfered with by the voluntary use of the arms. That is to say, the main swing around the spine and the two subsidiary swings around the shoulder joints become automatically synchronized. In consequence of this, there will be a greater number of accurately struck and therefore straight shots.

While it is true that accuracy of shot is an advantage to be gained from involuntary arm movement, this has to be weighed against the advantages to be gained by conscious arm movement, which are fourfold:

1. It probably makes you more aware of your arms, thus forming a link between your left shoulder and the grip.

2. It tends to stretch the arms, thus helping to keep the left one straight on the backswing and downward beyond impact: and then the right one.

3. It makes the hands go to a desirably higher level both on the backswing and on the forward swing.

4. It makes greater length probable.

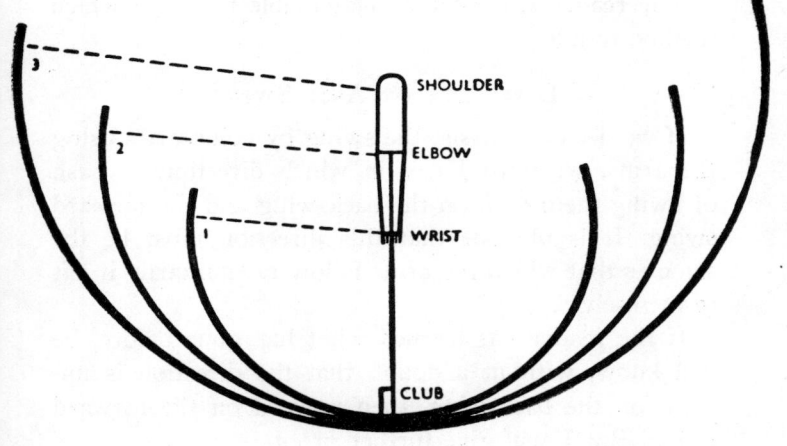

DIAGRAM 10. THE SHOULDER SWING

**1—CLUB ONLY, NARROW SWING 2—FOREARM AND CLUB, MEDIUM SWING
3—WHOLE ARM AND CLUB, WIDE SWING**

When studying the arm swing alone, it should be noted that a swing started by the hand must voluntarily bend the wrist and consequently be narrow. The desirable wide swing is produced by swinging the arm from its top end by means of the shoulder muscles. This applies to the left arm on the backswing and the right arm on the forward swing. Your hands should merely firmly grip the club shaft, thereby becoming "part of it." Centrifugal force will automatically cock and uncock your wrists. All wrist action should be automatic and involuntary.

The reader will later be better able to judge which method to adopt.

Direction of Arm Swing

If we decide to assist the swing by voluntarily using the arms, we must know in which direction to push or swing them both on the backswing and the forward swing. It is obvious that this direction must be the same as that which the arms follow involuntarily if left to themselves.

If the reader has learned what has gone before, he will know, without a doubt, that the direction is upward on the backswing, then upward on the forward swing. But I will give further proof.

It will be remembered that on the backswing the left shoulder goes down and to the right through a quarter of a circle; therefore, obviously, the hands must traverse a quarter of a circle to the right and upward.

It will also be remembered that we had to concentrate on the downward element of the shoulder movement; therefore, again obviously, we must concentrate on the upward part of the arm quarter circle. The downward movement of the left shoulder compels the left arm to move first to the right automatically; then the inevitable movement of the shoulder to the right allows the arm to go upward.

The mere fact that the left arm and the club are going to the right side of the body will automatically transfer all the weight that is necessary, whereas to concentrate on the movement of the arm to the right (as is implied by consciously taking the club head

THE GOLF SECRET—THIRD FACTOR 71

straight back behind the ball) would make you sway and shift the main hub position, or transfer too much weight and probably have the hands too low at the top of the backswing.

If the reader will go through these movements with a golf club, he will notice that the left shoulder going down helps the arm and club to go up, and vice versa. That is because these two movements are really in the same direction. They are on the same line, which will perhaps be better visualized as a groove.

I will again emphasize that all voluntary or conscious movement in the golf swing (or in any other muscular activity for that matter) must be in the same direction. See Diagram 11, in which are shown the club-head arc, the curve of which is due partly to subconscious wrist roll but mainly to subconscious turn of the shoulders on the hips; the actual hand arc, which will be less curved the more nearly horizontal the upper part of the spine; and also the feel of the hand arc, which, like the feel of the shoulder pivot, is in a straight line or nearly so.

Some people correctly push the left shoulder down, then mistakenly swing the club around themselves to the right, thus making the swing angular and necessitating an alteration in the direction of the force. Surely this is obviously wrong!

Therefore if you admit that the left shoulder should go down, you must also admit that the left arm and the club should go up.

Regarding the direction of the forward swing, this must be the reverse of the backswing. "Downswing"

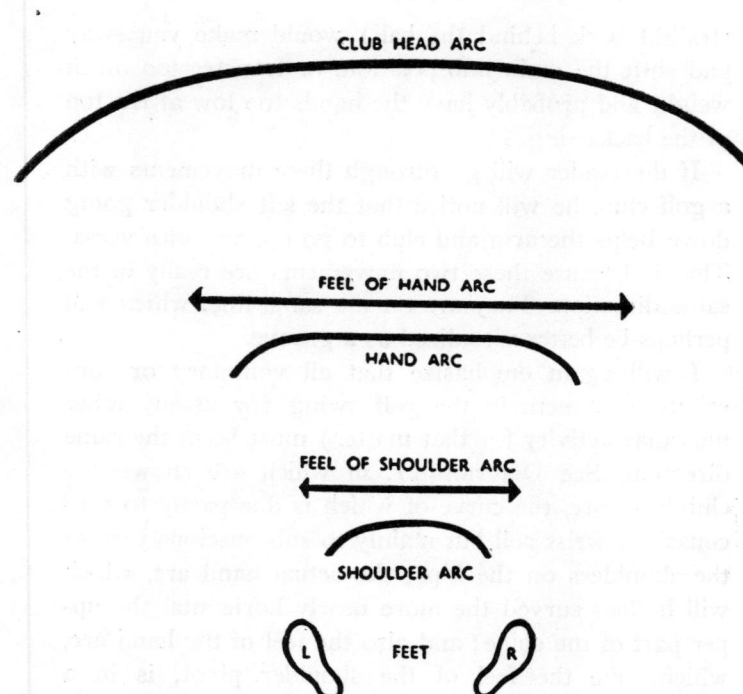

DIAGRAM 11. THE ARCS (OVERHEAD VIEW)

THE GOLF SECRET—THIRD FACTOR 73

is a misnomer that suggests finishing the shot at impact, and in fact, causes many players to do just that, and also to dip the body and hit the ground behind the ball.

As the left shoulder goes up, the hands and the club must come down; hence, the *down* stroke although you are swinging up. With irons the ball is contacted before the ground merely because it is behind the lowest point of the arc.

We have already satisfied ourselves that the left shoulder going upward leads the forward swing into the groove that it traversed on the backswing, and also causes the arms and the club to come down automatically into the hitting area.

It is from here that the active part of the forward swing actually begins—although you should think of it as beginning at the top—therefore the hit should follow the left shoulder, upward. Only thus can you keep the swing, as it should be, in a "straight" line.

There must be no pulling around the left side of the body, which may occur as a result of trying to swing parallel to the ground—*i.e.,* keeping the club head close to the ground—and which would keep the left shoulder too low at impact.

The feeling should be of trying to send the ball well above the target. In fact the higher you try to send the ball, the farther it will go. It will also go higher, but only toward the end of its trajectory since it is traveling uphill all the way, at right angles to the face of the club.

Most experts say that the club head is traveling its

fastest after impact. Surely the direction of the fastest movement—which soon after impact must be upward—must also be the direction of the forward swing. I know the fantastic view has been expressed that the club head floats onward faster after we have stopped hitting, but I cannot think that any intelligent man can accept that.

We must be hitting when the club head is traveling fastest—*i.e.,* after impact.

Diagram 12 shows the position of fastest speed of club head and also of arms and hands. The arms moving onward help to flatten the bottom of the arc even though the feel of the swing is upward. The speed of the onward-moving hands, together with the hitting upward, also keeps the face of the club square to the target during this period, thus delaying the automatic crossing of right hand over left until well after the ball has gone.

Finally, the left shoulder going upward and the hitting upward in the same direction, plus the fact that the left hand is higher than the right one on the club shaft, produce automatically the inside-to-out forward swing, which is almost universally considered desirable.

Expert Confirmation

1. There are in existence many photographs of experts at the top of the backswing, in which the left foot is merely rolled on to its inside edge, without any heel-raising at all. Try a backswing now, and see if you can get your left foot into that position by swinging your

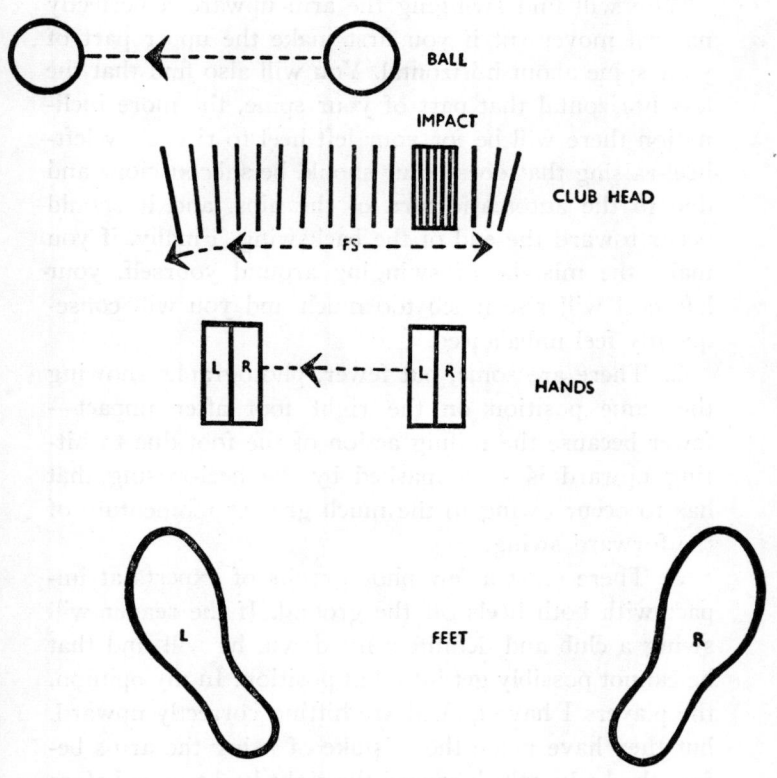

DIAGRAM 12. FASTEST CLUB-HEAD SPEED

FS—REGION OF FASTEST CLUB-HEAD SPEED

left arm in any other direction than upward. I know you cannot.

You will find swinging the arm upward a perfectly natural movement if you first make the upper part of your spine about horizontal. You will also find that the less horizontal that part of your spine, the more inclination there will be for your left heel to rise. Any left-heel-raising that does occur should be subconscious and due to the automatic turn of the hips, and it should occur toward the end of the backswing. Finally, if you make the mistake of swinging around yourself, your left heel will rise much too much and you will consequently feel unbalanced.

2. There are some, but fewer, photographs showing the same position on the right foot after impact—fewer because the rolling action of the foot due to hitting upward is soon masked by the heel-raising that has to occur owing to the much greater momentum of the forward swing.

3. There exist a few photographs of experts at impact with both heels off the ground. If the reader will swing a club and definitely hit down, he will find that he cannot possibly get into that position. In my opinion, the players I have quoted are hitting correctly upward, but they have made the mistake of using the arms before the body, which caused the right heel to rise before the body had pushed the left hip back and the left heel down.

4. At, or soon after, impact, in the case of most professionals the left shoulder is much higher than at address. That means that the left shoulder is going up-

THE GOLF SECRET—THIRD FACTOR

ward and is not turning left; therefore, the direction of the forward swing must be the same, that is, upward. In my opinion, some of the extreme examples of this nearly perpendicular line of the shoulders to be seen in photographs could not be maintained so far into the follow-through unless the forward swing were directly upward, as though an attempt was being made to hit the ball into the sky well above the target.

5. There are lots of photographs of experts, with the club head as much as twelve inches past impact position, that show (in addition to the above-mentioned shoulder line) a total absence of wrist roll and the club face square to the target, exactly as at impact. I maintain that this position of the hands and the club face one foot past impact is impossible to attain unless the player is hitting upward. Don't take my word for it . . . try now to get the club face into that position without hitting upward.

A modification of this impact position after impact is obtained when the player's wrists hinge instead of remaining firm, which is even more proof of hitting upward. There are several examples of this to be seen in golf books.

6. It is always said, "Let the club head follow the ball." Does the ball not go upward? How better can we let the club head follow the ball than to make it do so by hitting upward?

7. Many professionals say, let the driver contact the ball as the club head is rising. If you hit as the club head is rising, you must be hitting upward.

8. Some professionals admit to feeling no difference

in the swings with woods and irons, with which I entirely agree. This puts all clubs in the same category as the driver in No. 7 above so far as swinging upward is concerned. Of course, with irons the ball is contacted as the club head comes down, but merely because it is behind the bottom of the arc. The swing is not thereby affected.

9. Many professionals advocate the hands being high, both at the top of the backswing and after the forward swing—when the shot is finished. Surely for the hands to go high they must go upward, and what better method of ensuring their being high than to hit upward?

How to Do It

Having established the fact, I think, beyond doubt, that both the backswing and the forward swing must be upward, it now remains to show how to do it.

Grip a golf club with the left hand only, and without deliberately lowering the left shoulder, do a backswing from the shoulder joint—*i.e.,* swing straight up with the upper arm. Stop at the top and examine yourself. You will find that the left shoulder is too high, the shoulder pivot is incomplete, and the club shaft is above your neck and pointing to the left of the target.

Now repeat that backswing, using a downward motion of the left shoulder followed immediately by swinging the left arm from the shoulder joint, straight up. Stop at the top and again examine yourself. You will find the left shoulder low down and pointing over the ball, with a full shoulder pivot, and the club shaft

THE GOLF SECRET—THIRD FACTOR 79

above your right shoulder—*i.e.,* further back than before and pointing to the target. All these details are just as they should be.

Now repeat the backswing while gripping the club with both hands, but apart from gripping the club don't let the right arm do anything. That is, do the backswing entirely with the left shoulder and arm as before, and the right arm in all its parts will automatically assume its natural and correct position.

It will be remembered that on the backswing the arms are automatically carried nearly halfway up before the left arm starts its swing. How do I reconcile this with my advice to begin the arm swing immediately after the left shoulder begins to go down. The explanation is simple. It requires time for a thought to be transformed into action; therefore, if you delayed thinking of the arm swing until it should begin, you would be too late putting it into operation.

Conversely, by starting—*i.e.,* thinking of starting—the arm swing immediately after the left shoulder has put the main swing into the groove, you will commence the action rhythmically at the right time and place.

Apropos of this delayed action, it has recently been proved to be a fact. A Scotland Yard Inspector has invented a machine called an autotest car that proves that, when a motorist decides to apply the brake, one-third to half a second elapses before he does so, even in a dire emergency. Comparably, since it cannot take more than one second to perform the backswing, if you decide actively to swing up the left arm immediately after the left shoulder has started the backswing, you will not actually do so until the swing is about half completed.

As a matter of fact, after reasonable practice, when left-shoulder-down has become habitual, it may be feasible to think of both movements—left shoulder down and left arm up—as beginning together, since the two movements, being in the same direction, are inseparable.

All that has been said about the backswing, including the comparison with the autotest car-driver, applies equally to the forward swing. Therefore, begin the forward swing by pulling the left shoulder upward as quickly as possible until it has completed at least half a circle and is behind the neck.

Concurrently with this movement, the left-shoulder muscles acting on the left upper arm will automatically assist the swing since you have the intention to hit, and especially since your thoughts are concentrated on your left shoulder dominating the swing.

As the left shoulder begins to go upward into the groove, you should consciously, and with intent, hit upward with your right upper arm. Owing to the delayed action of maybe half a second, you will not actually hit until about halfway down—*i.e.,* in the hitting area—before which, of course, you could not hit upward.

The importance of thinking of hitting, and of thinking of speed, from the start of the forward swing will now be apparent. As with the backswing, it might prove desirable, with practice, to think of both movements—

THE GOLF SECRET—THIRD FACTOR

left shoulder up and hit upward with right upper arm—simultaneously.

Short Shots

All that I have said in this and the two preceding chapters refers in particular to any full shot with whatever club it is played—from a driver down through the spoon; to iron shots, including most shots from the rough; and even to a niblick explosion shot from a bunker. In all, by so doing, the club head will go "through" the ball.

Regarding part shots, or anything less than a full shot, maybe some elaboration is desirable.

I believe that every shot, from a drive to a putt, should be played, in effect, the same way. That is, the backswing should always be begun with a downward movement of the left shoulder and the forward swing always with an upward movement of the left shoulder. Further, I believe that every shot should be hit upward by the right arm immediately after the forward swing has commenced. By this means, the weight will always transfer as it should, much or little, automatically.

Think of all part shots as fractions of a drive, and if you wish to play a three-quarter, half, or quarter shot, do not try to do so by limiting the distance that your hands or the club head travel. That is too vague and will only result in hesitation and uncertainty, particularly as it necessitates transferring your attention from your left shoulder to your hands and the club and back again to the left shoulder, all in a split second. It cannot be done—successfully! Instead, always think of the left shoulder.

For a quarter shot let the shoulder go down a quarter of the way; for a half shot, halfway; and for a three-quarter shot, three-quarters of the way.

These distances cannot of course be gauged accurately, but they serve to demonstrate the principle of restricting all movements equally. That is to say, the shorter the shot, the less shoulder pivot and the less body movement generally. That is what professionals mean when they erroneously say, "No body movement with chip shots." Actually, the body movement should always be felt even if it is imperceptible to the onlookers. And don't forget that the only conscious, active movement is of the left shoulder (and maybe of the left upper arm on the backswing, and the right upper arm on the forward swing). All other movements—of hips, legs, feet, and including the desired limitation of the backswing—will occur subconsciously.

Remember also that with most of these part shots the forward swing should be practically the same as for a full shot because you are still hitting upward after impact just as with a full shot. Therefore, begin the forward swing by pulling the left shoulder up and let it uninterruptedly complete its half circle to behind the neck.

The exception to this rule would be the very short shot, say a chip or short pitch, which might be played slowly. There would then be no need for a full follow-through, but even so it would be wise to visualize that full finish, thus to ensure the left shoulder and consequently the club head traversing the correct arc.

As with full shots, the right arm should come in at the right time—*i.e.,* after the left shoulder has determined the groove.

Many players prefer to play very short shots all right-handed. While it is true that the shorter the shot the less harm there will be from doing this because the hands are not above the hitting area where the right arm should come in, nevertheless many shots are fluffed by concentrating on the right side of the body because this tends to delay or prevent weight transference to the left.

With all these short shots, including putts, much better results will be obtained by concentrating on the left shoulder to begin the forward swing. Then all the body will be moving, as it should be, however slightly, in the same direction.

To some people, concentration on the left shoulder will no doubt seem too remote from the club head for very short shots. For them, the rule to hit upward with the right arm (or hand, if they prefer to think of it that way), must be doubly remembered because the left shoulder will not then be leading the swing into the correct groove. Instead, the right arm—if the blow is upward—will tend to push the left shoulder into the groove; also, there will be only little danger because the left shoulder will have come down only slightly.

Incidentally, it is this almost imperceptible movement of the left shoulder, and consequently of the body also, that is the cause of some professionals believing that there is no body movement in putting. They are wrong.

The third factor of the Golf Secret is the sensation of swinging directly upward, both on the backswing and on the forward swing, the left shoulder being assisted by the left- and right-shoulder muscles swinging the upper arms, either subconsciously or consciously.

Chapter 4

GOLF FALLACIES—IN TRUE LIGHT

Use and Misuse of—
Words
The Mind
The Body
The Head
The Legs and Feet
The Arms
The Hands
The Fairway

In describing the three factors of the golf secret, I have intentionally omitted many details of what happens during the course of the swing—such as wrist-cocking, stopping at the top, and timing—so as not to confuse the issue.

Among the missing links now to be considered, some have already been touched upon where appropriate, while most have hitherto been considered to be controversial matters—even by the experts—and consequently have contributed to the prevalent contradictory teaching.

If you swing as I have described, most of the do's and don'ts of golf can be forgotten. The do's will occur automatically. The don'ts will not happen.

Use and Misuse of Words

This involves criticism of the expressions "backswing," "downswing," "hitting down," and "follow-through." According to my beliefs, none of these gives the correct impression of what a golfer is trying to do.

A golf club swung backward and forward by a person in the correct golfing attitude describes approximately a circle, going up to the right and up to the left, with the greatest force in both cases past the bottom of the arc. That is, it is the same on both sides of the address position. So why use different names that suggest that the force is applied in different positions and directions?

The simplest, most apt, and most descriptive terms are "right upswing" and "left upswing."

These expressions describe exactly what the player should feel he wishes and intends to do.

"Backswing" suggests—and causes—either too rotatory and too flat swinging around the entire body; or swinging too far straight back on the reverse target line, tending to cause swaying, too much weight transference, and too upright a swing.

"Downswing" suggests—and causes—hitting downward and staying down, and probably lurching, because the left shoulder has not been got out of the way. Also, the shot tends to finish soon after impact, like a tennis chop shot. Other possible results are: staying on the right leg and hitting the ground behind the ball, or coming from outside the line, thus pulling the ball to the left, or slicing it.

"Hitting down" with iron clubs produces the same wrong impressions and faults as "downswing."

With iron clubs the ball *is* hit as the club head comes down, but simply because it is behind the bottom of the arc. The forward swing is not thereby altered, but is still upward.

Many professional writers now use the term "forward swing" instead of "downswing." They, at least, are moving in the right direction, but they haven't gone far enough. I would go further and say "left upswing."

"Follow-through" ceases to have any meaning if you think of "left upswing," since it then becomes what it really is, an inevitable part of the correct forward swing.

While registering my disapproval of the terms in common usage because they are harmful, I have used the terms "backswing" and "forward swing" so as to avoid confusion in reading. "Downswing" and "hitting down" I will not use.

Use and Misuse of the Mind

This involves considerations of relaxation, concentration, and tension.

In most golf books, in my opinion, there is a lot of misinformed talk about these subjects. Briefly, they all say, "relax and concentrate but have no tension."

As I understand the meaning of these words, nobody can relax and concentrate at the same time; nor can anyone concentrate without tension. In fact these two are almost synonymous.

Relaxation implies a lessening of voluntary bodily and mental function—*i.e.,* soft muscles and a blank mind.

Concentration calls for the opposite qualities—a

sense of alertness of body and mind, in consequence of which the person is, of necessity, in a state of tension.

To say "relax and concentrate" is comparable to commanding a horse to "whoa, gee-up."

It is a fact that before any muscular effort the muscles to be used become taut, or acquire tension. For example, there is a long, slender muscle in the calf of the leg, which commonly snaps in tennis players if, caught unawares—*i.e.,* relaxed—they make a sudden effort to retrieve the ball. That is why a tennis player should be always alert, on the *qui vive,* tense, concentrating—anything but relaxed—and literally "on his toes."

Another example of concentration or tension is the indignant hero in a novel who clenches his fists and teeth and sets his jaw. I am sure that actors are taught to do these things when portraying anger.

This anger is closely allied to the concentration needed in golf. Aren't you, in a way, annoyed with the golf ball when wishing to hit it hard? And have you ever felt relaxed when annoyed or angry? No, annoyance, anger, or concentration has the opposite effect: it produces tension, a tautening of muscles, and a desirable firmer grip. At least one professional has written, in effect, that annoyance can improve golf. That has also been my experience, and I believe it is due to the consequent increased tension-concentration and the accompanying firmer grip.

As a final example, most people must have noticed when reading an exciting book, or watching a thrilling film, how through concentration their whole body becomes tense, their muscles contracted, their heart beating stronger and faster, even to the extent of causing headache and later preventing sleep.

It is beyond my comprehension how anybody can believe that a relaxed body can propel a golf ball three hundred yards. Also, the facial contortions of many professionals when wielding a golf club suggest to me a very high degree of tension.

Concentrate at golf you must—as with any other purposeful activity. A very firm grip is the key to concentration.

Use and Misuse of the Body

This calls for comment on the shape of the body at address, the backswing, the forward swing, the inside-to-out forward swing, pressing, the stop at the top, timing, and golf exercises.

Shape of the Body. Professional writers often say, "Stand erect," "Don't stoop," or "There must be no overhanging of the upper part of the body." But Diagram 4 plainly shows that most experts have the upper part of their spines about horizontal at address.

Shape of the Swing. Whether the swing is flat or upright should depend entirely on the degree of back-bending. The more nearly horizontal the upper part of the spine, the more upright the swing. That is why the swing with short clubs is more upright than with long ones.

Also, that is why the swing should always feel the same. There should be no deliberate attempt to swing more upright or more flat. Merely swing correctly by revolving the shoulders.

Backswing. The backswing should be begun by the left shoulder moving the body, assisted actively or subconsciously by the left arm through the shoulder muscles, thus setting the hub (upper spine) in motion.

Forward Swing. The forward swing should be begun by the left shoulder moving the body, assisted subconsciously by both arms—maybe consciously by the right one—through the shoulder muscles. The forward swing, like the backswing, is essentially a revolving of the shoulders around the horizontal upper part of the spine.

Inside-to-out Forward Swing. Providing the body and the swing are the correct shape, as already described, and the swing is correctly executed, then the forward swing will be, inevitably, from inside-to-out, without the player trying to make it so.

If both hands were at the same level on the club shaft, then the backswing and the forward swing would be identical and "parallel" to the target line. But because the left hand is higher, so is the left shoulder, which produces a slight curving of the left side of the body. This anatomical adjustment compels the backswing to come somewhat inside the line; then if the forward swing is performed correctly by pulling the left shoulder upward and hitting upward, it is bound to be inside-to-out.

Therefore to make a conscious effort to swing from inside-to-out is to court disaster since you will then swing too much inside-to-out.

GOLF FALLACIES—IN TRUE LIGHT 91

Pressing. Professionals and their books almost invariably say, "Don't press," which can only mean "Don't hit hard." This mistaken advice comes from a wrong conception of the direction of the hit. Hitting downward or even forward when pressing, or hitting hard, causes lurching and movement of the head to the left. But if the swing is visualized as a circle, and moving fastest after impact, which will necessitate hitting upward, then you can, and should, press—*i.e.,* hit as hard as you can.

By pulling the left shoulder up and then to the right through its half circle, thus getting the left shoulder out of the way, all the pressing you can produce can do no harm.

Many years ago I asked Charles Ward to tell me the "secret." He replied, "Just hit the ball hard." He won the 1950 *Daily Mail* Tournament, beating Bobby Locke in the play-off!

I am sure there has been too much gentle golf taught, and the wrong impression given by such mistaken expressions as "grip lightly," "no tension," and "swing slowly and let the club head do the work." I believe such teaching belongs to the day when tennis was lawn tennis, and table tennis was ping-pong. Both these games are now aggressive, as I believe golf should be.

It is time for a little of "grip the club as tightly as you feel you should to knock the ball out of sight." I recommend this hard hitting even for the beginner.

The Stop at the Top. Should there be a conscious stop at the top of the backswing? Yes, definitely! All are bound to agree that it is impossible to reverse an automobile or to make anything else change its direction without first stopping, if only momentarily. The same rule applies to a golf club.

But the golf swing, as distinct from the golf club, needs a little more consideration. I am quite sure that at no time during the full golf swing does the entire body and the golf club become stationary, but all the different parts of this ensemble stop in a very definite order.

The backswing having begun, the left shoulder is the first part to stop, when it should be in front of the neck; then the whole of the left arm, from shoulder to wrist, stops; then the hand stops on completion of wrist-cocking; and, finally, the club head stops when the impetus of the swing has bent the club shaft.

While, say, momentum is still causing the hand to cock the wrist, the left shoulder is beginning the forward swing by going upward into its half-circle groove, and the left hip is moving to the left and backward, by which time the hands have automatically come down into, or toward, the hitting area, with the wrists by now fully cocked or just starting to uncock automatically, the club shaft being by now fully bent.

That is to say, the order in which these four parts stop prior to reversing, at the end of their individual backswings, is the same as the order in which they started it: left shoulder, arm, hand, club head.

There are three very obvious reasons for this order:

1. One would expect the finish to be in the same

GOLF FALLACIES—IN TRUE LIGHT 93

order as the beginning because the earlier starters have a start on the others.

2. The relative distances the four parts have to travel on the backswing would make it likely that the shorter journey of the shoulder would end first.

3. By no other order of stopping at the top could you get rhythm into the swing. Obviously, the first part to stop must be the first part to start again in the reverse direction. Also, these four points of pressure in developing the speed of the forward swing must be applied in sequence, beginning with the leading part, the left shoulder.

Visualizing these occurrences, it is plain to see how the speed of the forward swing is gradually though automatically built up and increased, and that the player must not interfere with the rhythm by attempting to increase the speed at any given point, as is so often erroneously advocated. It is also plain to see why chaos results from "pulling on the rope from the middle" by starting the forward swing with arm or hand.

Until it becomes second nature to do a full shoulder pivot by forcing the left shoulder downward through its quarter circle, there is a way by which you can be sure of completing the movement and also of ensuring the correct stop at the top.

When you are commencing the backswing, while you are looking at the ball, the left shoulder gradually comes into the field of vision. That is to say, if you think about it, you can see the shoulder without taking your eyes off the ball: and you can actually see when it stops, before which you should not begin the forward swing.

You would probably not attempt this feat when actually playing, but I can assure you it is well worth while when practicing.

When playing part shots or short shots, whether with short clubs or with the hands down the stick, there is a very important point regarding the length of time to stop at the top. I think it will be agreed that the longer the backswing, the greater the momentum! Therefore, in a short shot there will be less momentum and, consequently, a longer time will be required for the automatic wrist-cocking which the momentum produces. Consideration and understanding of these facts lead us naturally to the formation of a rule which will greatly improve anybody's "short" game: *The shorter the shot, the longer the stop.*

It is impossible to give details of how long to stop, but on very short shots, including putts, I believe it is best to determine not to begin the forward swing until the entire backswing, including that of the wrists and the club head, is complete, and therefore all backward movement is stopped.

In my opinion, this waiting for the wrists to cock is a much better and safer method than deliberately cocking the wrists as advocated by many professionals. Conscious wrist-cocking is wrong; it introduces a different movement into the swing, since it must be done with the hands; therefore it makes the game needlessly more difficult—and produces too much wrist-cocking. It is a mistake to aim at a lot of wrist-cocking for a short shot. Every movement will be automatically reduced in proportion to the length of backswing.

Finally, when playing any shot, even a full one, if a player experiences difficulty in starting the forward swing with the left shoulder before the other parts of the backswing are completed, he will be well advised to make a deliberate, though momentary, stop at the end of the entire backswing rather than feel that there is no stop—so long as he does begin the forward swing with the left shoulder. Indeed, if you are past the first blush of youth, you will probably get better results by this method of regarding the backswing and the forward swing as two separate entities.

Timing. A beloved word of the professionals is "timing," but they usually wrap it in mystery. I have not seen it correctly defined, much less explained. As I see it, timing is best described as rhythm, easy to understand and easily acquired. We will consider it under three headings:

1. There must be synchronization of the two arm swings with the body swing through the three hubs—*i.e.,* the two shoulder joints and the upper part of the spine. This will include the undoing of all joint-cocking at impact. Visualize the uncocking, or unwinding, of the wrists, also of the left elbow joint if bent, and the left shoulder carrying the left arm down on the forward swing.

I will anticipate the reader's question: How is this to be achieved? It will all happen automatically if you obey my second injunction below and allow the upper arms to come into the shot subconsciously, although with practice you might assist voluntarily with the right upper arm.

2. Get rhythm into the swing by beginning it with the leading part, the left shoulder.

3. The time relationship between the backswing and the forward swing is most important in producing rhythm, so we will consider this in some detail. Players are usually told to swing back slowly, but it has often been observed that most experts do not swing back slowly. True enough, many don't; but if they swing back quickly, they swing forward even more quickly, and that is why they drive the ball prodigious distances. There must be that difference in speed on the backswing and the forward swing.

Now we can see that this correct time relationship between the back and forward swings, in conjunction with concentration on the left shoulder, produces rhythm, which in turn produces synchronization of the three swings and therefore good timing.

The best example of good timing to watch is a child (preferably over five years of age) throwing a stone into the sea. He doesn't think of when his wrist cocks or uncocks! Watch how the body turns first, and how much more quickly the arm comes forward than it went back.

In parenthesis, the average woman throws a stone only a few yards from her right shoulder joint—and misses the target! Any man can throw a stone; we all learned as boys. Women golfers please note! Try it now, and note the different speeds of the back and forward swings. Note also the definite stop at the top before the throw—*i.e.,* the forward swing. Also notice that your body begins to move and weight to transfer, without consciously using your legs, before the arm comes forward. Lastly, notice that you don't give your wrist a thought.

If, when playing golf, you find that you are mistiming your shots, you can easily recall this rhythm, even without your opponent's knowing what you are doing.

As you walk around the course, swing a club with your right hand only, as though you were throwing a stone, but "throw it away" upward. You will then soon be timing your shots correctly.

Golf Exercises. The most important exercise to a golfer who values his health is one that counteracts the deformities that golf tends to cause.

When the left shoulder is permanently higher than the right one, it usually signifies a lateral curvature of the spine called "scoliosis."

Round shoulders indicate an increase in the normal forward curve of that part of the spine, the condition called "kyphosis." As kyphosis increases, it tends to obliterate the normal forward lumbar curve of the spine at waist level.

Any such spinal deformity renders the development of osteoarthritis of the spine, which is painful and incapacitating, more likely in later life. The deformity causes the arthritis by improper or imperfect alignment of adjacent joint surfaces.

The exercises to be described are simple and consist of bending your body in the opposite direction to which golf tends to bend it.

To counteract the high left shoulder of the address and impact positions, stand erect, put your right arm straight above your head and push the left arm down by the side of the left leg as far as you can, so that the two arms form practically one perpendicular line. Do the right side too, but concentrate on the left side.

To counteract the round shoulders that tend to develop in regular players who correctly bend their backs, bend your whole body backward into the opposite position to the crouching attitude of golf.

First twist your arms outward; then push your shoulders backward; then bend your neck by pushing your head as far back as you can; then bend the upper part of your spine backward so that your chest comes up and forward; and then go as far back as you can, thus increasing the normal lumbar curve. Incidentally, this exercise will increase your chest measurement and reduce your waist measurement, but it will not, of course, improve your golf, except in so far as you may feel better from having a better carriage.

As a matter of fact you will probably play better golf by allowing the deformities to develop because you will then more easily drop into the address position; but it will be a different story when the arthritis ensues.

The most important, and probably the most difficult movement in golf, is to get a full shoulder pivot with only little movement of the head.

GOLF FALLACIES—IN TRUE LIGHT 99

It follows, therefore, that the most important exercise to improve golf is to twist the upper part of the spine, including the part in the neck.

Turn your head to look alternately over your left and right shoulders. At first, do it slowly, forcing your head as far around as you can, and try gradually to increase the range. Later, do it quickly as it should happen in the golf swing. Then, do it the other way around —*i.e.,* keep your head still and turn your shoulders as you did your head.

Now, do the same thing while standing in the golfing attitude, always thinking of left-shoulder-down and up. At first do it slowly, forcing alternately the left and right shoulders under the chin; then do it in the proper golf swing tempo.

At this stage incorporate the arms by pushing the left upper arm up from the shoulder joint as the left shoulder goes down, then the right upper arm up from the shoulder joint as the left shoulder goes up.

Lastly, repeat the exercise while gripping a golf club, but do grip it tightly.

Incidentally, I would ask you to notice how the wrists function when you don't think about them but think only of your left shoulder.

You will notice that the variations of this simple exercise are constructive in that they improve your swing at the same time as they exercise. They also, incidentally, give your arms and legs all the exercise they need.

The second important golf exercise is of the muscles of your hands and especially those of the forearms with which you grip the club. For that, you need only grip the club shaft while doing the other exercise, but do grip it with all the strength you possess.

It boils down to this—the best exercise for golf is golf, but it must be correct golf so as to train and develop the correct muscles and also the correct feel of the swing.

USE AND MISUSE OF THE HEAD

This involves discussion of eye-on-the-ball, head-turning, head-still, head-down, head-up, topping, and slicing. These attributes and faults are inseparable in discussion, and so will be considered together to avoid repetition.

Actually, if you make the upper part of your spine horizontal and swing by revolving your shoulders around it as already instructed, then the attributes will be yours and the faults will not happen.

Head-still, head-down, head-up, topping, and slicing can all be disposed of very briefly for the following reasons:

1. The head cannot be held still because it must turn, first to the right and then to the left. Otherwise you will restrict the backswing and the forward swing.

2. Holding down the head to prevent head-up will also prevent it from turning, so it must not be *held* down. Swing as instructed and it will *stay* down.

3. Head-up is chiefly due to standing too erect. With proper back-bending a player is much more likely to turn his head on its own axis than be guilty of head-up. Even if this turning is done too early, in the play-

er's anxiety to see where the ball is going, it will not raise the head or the arc of the swing. Therefore, he is much less likely to top or slice the ball.

When head-up occurs, the upper part of the body, including the hands and therefore also the club-head arc, also comes up; consequently, the ball is topped, or missed. Alternatively, if the head goes up earlier in the forward swing, the left shoulder will turn to the left throwing the club head across the "line," which, since the club head comes to the ball from outside-to-in, will produce a slice.

So bend your back and you will practically have beaten the two commonest and most disastrous faults in golf.

Regarding head-turning, as previously stated, to get the very important full shoulder pivot on the backswing, you must either let your left shoulder push your head around on its axis or turn it to the right before beginning the backswing.

In the pushing method, when the upper part of the spine, including that in the neck, is fully twisted, it must be obvious that, if the head is not allowed to turn, a full shoulder pivot is impossible. On the forward swing the same thing applies. When the right shoulder is approaching the chin, the upper spine being tightly twisted, the head must turn to the left. Again it must be obvious that, if you do hold your head back (head-down, head-still, or eye-on-the-ball too long), it is bound to act as a brake on the forward swing by restricting the shoulder turn.

If you turn the head to the right (pointing the chin,

as it is called) before you start the backswing, you really put your head into the position where your left shoulder would have pushed it. Therefore, by this method you can get a full shoulder pivot without further movement of the head to the right. That is the reason for this maneuver, and not any of the other peculiar suggestions that have been made. I have even read that it is done to enable you to look at the ball with your left eye! You should see the ball with both eyes.

To make sure that you are seeing the ball with both eyes, address the ball, turn your head to the right, then shut your left eye. If you cannot then see the ball, it means that your nose is in the line of vision of your right eye and that you have turned your head too far to the right. Therefore turn it back until you can see the ball. The higher the bridge of your nose, the less you will be able to turn your head to the right and still see the ball with your right eye.

A little explanation will enable the reader to understand how important it is to see the ball with both eyes. When we look at any object—for example, a golf ball—with both eyes (binocular vision), the image seen with one eye is superimposed "on top of" the image seen with the other eye. That is to say, we see two separate images, and if one does not "fit" exactly on top of the other, we are seeing double. It is this superimposed image that gives the object body, or depth, or perspective.

Now if we look at the same object with one eye

(monocular vision), the image appears to be flatter, or loses perspective. A golf ball would look more like a disk. It will now be apparent why we must see the ball with both eyes.

To drive the lesson home, I will relate the story of the one-eyed billiard player whose biggest break was five. He challenged a friend who often got a break of fifty, to a match. The better player had to bandage one eye. The bet was on, and very soon the player with the bandaged eye was even missing the cue ball.

If any doubting Thomas reads this, I invite him to try it. I would back any one-eyed snooker player to beat Joe Davis with one eye bandaged. Comparably, it would be a safe bet that any one-armed sixteen-handicap golfer would beat even Henry Cotton, if Cotton played with one arm.

Once again then, the rule is to bend your back; then your eyes will be wide open, and your head will stay down naturally; consequently, you will see the ball plainly and your head will turn naturally, so that there will be only little, if any, tendency for your head to spoil the shot.

All you need do then is think that you see the ball hit. You will probably blink and not see it, but it doesn't matter.

Use and Misuse of the Legs and Feet

This calls for brief consideration of the set, the forward press, the pivot, left-heel-raising, weight transference, balance, left-hip-back, left-side-out-of-the-way, left-heel-down, and firm-left-leg. All these movements are relatively unimportant because they happen automatically if the swing is performed as described.

The Set. The set refers to the general setup of the body at address, and is entirely due to the left hand's being higher than the right one on the club shaft. Prove this by standing in the golfing attitude with your hands palm to palm opposite your middle. Now, keeping the left arm straight, push the right hand down until its palm is in contact with your left fingers.

What has happened? Your hands have moved to the left opposite the inside of the left leg. Weight has transferred slightly to the left. The right knee, hip, and shoulder have gone down and a little forward, while your left knee, hip, and shoulder have gone up and a little backward.

That is the set, and the position at impact is merely a live replica of it.

The set is a naturally assumed position and not merely a bending inward of the right knee after assuming the stance.

The set is not so apparent in golfers who have the left hand less on top of the shaft and who consequently play the ball nearer the middle of the stance and usually use a flatter swing with a quicker turn of the wrists after impact. In other words, the more to the left you play the ball, the more pronounced the set.

The Forward Press. The forward press is merely a slight increase of the set to the left before beginning the backswing.

It is usually said that the forward press should begin

GOLF FALLACIES—IN TRUE LIGHT 105

with the hands or the right knee, with which opinion I disagree because there is a tendency to push the knee toward the ball and consequently to swing too flat and too rotatorily. Also, it necessitates transference of the player's attention from one part of his anatomy to another during the swing.

If you must use the forward press, do it by slightly raising the left shoulder. Then you will be concentrating on the same part with which you are going to begin the backswing, and by so doing, see how your hands move straight to the left and not in a curve. By this method you will conform to my belief—which we have proved—that all movements below the chest are involuntary.

The forward press has been seen to occur by means of slow-motion photography, but nevertheless it should *not* be made a voluntary movement. A boy does it when throwing a stone, but he is not aware of it.

Why become aware of it at golf? It is a natural subconscious movement that will vary in degree with different people. The natural conscious preparation to hit a golf ball—or anything else—is the backswing. Do just that, and the forward press will take care of itself, though maybe imperceptibly.

The Pivot. The pivot as usually taught is a rotation of the whole body by voluntary leg movements, which is wrong in principle and causes swinging around, too flat.

The pivot is an inevitable accompaniment of the swing but should be allowed to happen automatically, not be voluntarily forced into unnatural and varying paths. In fact, the word "pivot" itself, together with any thought of pivoting, should be deleted from the golfer's vocabulary—unless it be transferred to the shoulders.

Some professionals do now speak of the "shoulder pivot," but even that designation is not correct and gives a totally wrong impression since the shoulder movement is more complicated.

You may remember that you feel only that you push the left shoulder down, then pull it up, but that while you are doing that, both shoulders are automatically revolved (or turned) by the subconscious movement of the hips.

Left-heel-raising. The left heel should not be voluntarily raised at all. Whatever does happen will be secondary to movement elsewhere. The more upright the swing, the less the heel will rise. In a correctly executed backswing the pressure should first be felt to pass to the inside edge of the left foot. Any subsequent heel-raising is merely to accommodate the later stages of a full backswing and is due to the automatic turn of the hips. That is why professionals say that in short shots any left-foot movement is felt rather than seen.

Weight Transference. Golf books often instruct the reader to transfer his weight to the right on the backswing, then to the left on the forward swing. This is entirely wrong, as voluntary transference of weight is bound to be carried too far.

Weight transference is involuntary and automatic with any purposeful movement of the upper part of

GOLF FALLACIES—IN TRUE LIGHT 107

the body, and it is entirely for the purpose of subconsciously maintaining balance.

Reach to one side to pick up a book, then stop and see how your weight has transferred even without your knowledge, much less your assistance. Do the same thing again by intentionally transferring your weight with your legs, and you will probably topple over.

In the golf swing, the mere swinging of the club to the right or left side of the body—even though it feels to be going directly upward—will automatically transfer exactly the amount of weight that is necessary, if you don't interfere.

Balance. Balance is very important and is often said to be the most noticeable feature of professional golf. It will be difficult to attain if the swing is wrong or if the weight is *consciously* moved from heel to toe, or for that matter in any direction.

But if the swing feels to be in a straight line, up to the right and then up to the left by conscious shoulder movement as described—leaving the legs to find subconsciously their correct positions—then maintenance of balance will be simple, natural, and in fact inevitable.

Left-hip-back. To begin the forward swing by pushing the left hip backward would necessitate transferring your attention from one part of the body to another and back again during the split second available. Impracticable and unnecessary, as well as catastrophic!

If attempted, the whole body would revolve to the left, throwing the club across the line and causing a slice. To me this seems, and is, so obvious that I find it hard to believe that some eminent professionals advocate this method to ensure an inside-to-out swing. Don't accept anyone's statement however eminent he may be. Try it for yourself. I know what will happen —you will start to think for yourself. I wish golfers would!

Slow-motion photography is responsible for this fallacy, too, because it shows that apparently the left hip does move first; but what is overlooked is that this is a preparatory, involuntary movement, caused by the conscious movement of the upper part of the body that wields the implement. That we have proved.

Watch an expert crack a long whip across the front of his body, and you will plainly see the quick jerk of the hips to the left to be apparently the first movement, although it was probably preceded by an imperceptible shoulder movement.

But crack a whip violently yourself, and you will be conscious of using only the upper part of your body.

Therefore execute the forward swing with your left shoulder, and the left hip will go back as, and when, it should to maintain your balance.

Left-side-out-of-the-way. Golfers are told to get the left side out of the way voluntarily, but the side, like the left hip, will take care of itself if the swing is right. To attempt it pulls the whole body around to the left.

Left-heel-down. Pushing the left heel down as a first movement is often erroneously advocated. This again is automatic, the heel being pushed down by the left hip going backward, which in turn is due to the voluntary movement of the upper part of the body.

Firm-left-leg. This is said to be essential for a good shot and probably is. I believe that Ossie Pickworth's bent leg at impact is nonetheless firm though not straight.

Since the left foot when firmly on the ground becomes the fulcrum of the forward swing, it might be wondered why a good shot can sometimes be played with the left heel off the ground or with the left knee bent at impact. The explanation is simple. The front part of the foot can be the fulcrum, the foot or leg—though "kinked"—being held firm by contracted muscles.

The explanation of the cause of these two faults is equally simple. The left heel off the ground at impact implies too late or insufficient weight transference due to hitting with the arms instead of first applying the body on the forward swing. The bent left knee at impact means that the swing was set lower down by excessive knee-bending at address.

It is not possible to transfer your thoughts from the swing to make your left leg firm, then back again. In any case it is unnecessary because the left leg becomes firm automatically by the stretching of the whole left side of the body, which is due to the left shoulder's being pulled up and the consequent backward movement of the left hip.

It will be appreciated then, that the forward press, the pivot, left-heel-raising, weight transference, balance, left-hip-back, left-side-out-of-the-way, left-heel-down, and firm-left-leg are all automatic, subconscious movements, activated by simply revolving the shoulders around the horizontal upper part of the spine.

Use and Misuse of the Arms

This involves discussion of right-elbow-down, straight-left-arm, backswing, pull-down-with-left-arm, hitting down with irons, and hitting late.

Right-elbow-down. Among the golf stars, the only one I know of whose right elbow is allowed to go very high on the backswing is James Bruen; therefore, he may be a law unto himself. At the same time I think it can be more easily explained than is usually thought. He is said to have an unusually high finish and so must hit definitely upward. Also his hands are very high at the top of the backswing, in which position his right elbow would have to go up if his backswing were excessively upright, which I suspect it is. A top-of-backswing photograph of him in Henry Cotton's book shows the club shaft to be well short of the horizontal despite the height of his hands. This can only mean a very firm grip and firm wrists with minimum wrist-cocking.

It seems to me that the sum total of all this is that he plays golf in the same manner that I am trying to prove that most professionals do—only he does more so!

Since I am trying to show the easy road to good golf, we will not emulate Mr. Bruen's extreme though correct swing.

Right-elbow-down does not mean that the elbow must be held consciously against the body but merely that it should not lead the way and go upward, which, incidentally, it will tend to do if the right hand is under the shaft. Also, it does not mean that the elbow must be perpendicularly under the shaft at the top of the backswing; which could happen only if the left wrist were well rolled over on the way up. That wrist-rolling is not only unnecessary but undesirable.

If the backswing is performed by the left shoulder as instructed, and maybe assisted by the left upper arm only, then all that is meant by right-elbow-down will happen automatically. Therefore it is merely another of those golf maxims that can be forgotten.

Straight left arm. While most professionals do maintain a straight left arm on the backswing, it is still debatable whether they would play as well if they did not. For instance the late, and great, Harry Vardon always allowed his left arm to bend on the backswing and even deprecated a straight one. Henry Cotton says that he might emulate Vardon but finds it more difficult than keeping the arm straight. Is it possible that professionals—not to mention the unfortunate amateurs—have trained themselves for years to maintain an unnaturally straight arm that is unnecessary?

Careful examination of photographs of professionals at the top of the backswing will reveal that many of them, and even some who claim to have a straight left arm, have in fact a slight bend at the elbow.

I believe that the important thing is that the left arm should be firm—which it can be only if the grip is very firm—and then it will be relatively and sufficiently straight.

It seems to me that if you can maintain a straight left arm, there may be something gained, such as a definitely wide swing, and absence of the necessity to straighten the arm on the way down. But if you find it difficult, you will probably play better without it, especially if you convince yourself that it is unnecessary.

I am certain of one thing: you cannot keep the left arm straight if you swing the club back with your hand. Any use of the hand must soon bend the wrist, and the next natural thing to happen is for the elbow to bend.

That is why I am also certain that straight-left-armed professionals do not start the backswing with the hand, even if they think and say they do.

I think all experts are agreed that a straight left arm at impact is essential, but there is at least one notable exception to even this rule. Babe Didrickson Zaharias, recent woman champion of the United States and Great Britain, has photographs of herself in her book, *Championship Golf,* showing a bent left arm not only at the top of the backswing but also at impact, and also after impact with the elbow leading.

I am inclined to think that, at impact as at the top, firmness may be more important than straightness. Of course a firm straight arm has the advantage of providing a radius of fixed length, whereas a firm bent arm provides a radius that might vary in length.

Presuming that a straight left arm is desirable at the top and at impact, there are four factors concerned in its production and maintenance:

1. The player's build.

GOLF FALLACIES—IN TRUE LIGHT

2. Firmly contracted forearm muscles.

3. Stretching of left arm to separate wrist from shoulder.

4. Beginning of the backswing and forward swing by the left shoulder, as instructed.

We will now consider the effects of these factors:

1. Generally speaking, slim, narrow-chested people will find it easier to maintain a straight left arm both at the top and at impact than fleshy, broad-shouldered people.

2. The muscles about the elbow joint are those of the forearm, which become firm when we grip anything. Therefore, the more tightly we grip the club shaft, the firmer these muscles will be and the more definitely they will splint the elbow joint and prevent its movement. That statement can be proved by doing a backswing with the left arm, first with the hand open and then with it tightly clenched, noticing the different behavior of the elbow joint.

3. Repeat those two backswings with the hand alternately open and clenched, but also stretch the arm before starting. I think you will find this helps to keep the arm straight.

4. If you add to the above three factors a last, beginning of a proper backswing by a downward motion of the left shoulder, you will find it much easier to keep the left arm straight. The reason for this is that the shoulder going down carries or pushes the arm from its top end, so the arm has no reason to bend; whereas if you started the backswing with your hand or even arm, the arm would have to drag the shoulder after it,

thus producing a further tendency to bending in addition to that already described as due to using the hand.

After the downward-moving shoulder has carried the straight left arm a good way up, the upper arm may either subconsciously or consciously (you will remember) assist the action. It is the conscious use of the arm that might tend to bend it, but it must be obvious to everyone that swinging the arm by the muscles above the elbow will have less tendency to bend the elbow than using muscles below it—*i.e.,* those of the forearm or hand.

Regarding the straight left arm at impact, I believe that, in addition to the recommended firmness of arm and grip, the most important factor is the left shoulder going upward into its half-circle groove on the forward swing, thus getting out of the way and leaving room for the long straight left arm. The reader will remember that in effect the left arm is longer than the right owing to the left hand's being higher on the shaft. Therefore, it should not be difficult to visualize that, if the left shoulder is not high enough at impact, then the left elbow will have to be bent to shorten the distance between shoulder and club head so that the club head is able to contact the ball.

Backswing. One need say no more about the futility of beginning the backswing with the arm than has been said under "Straight-left-arm," except perhaps to remind you that to do so is to make the shoulder joint the hub, which is movable, instead of the upper part of the spine, which is a fixed hub that merely turns on its

GOLF FALLACIES—IN TRUE LIGHT 115

axis. It does not require a King Solomon to make the wise and correct choice.

Hitting Down with Irons. The word "down" implies performing the forward swing with some portion of the arm or arms. To hit down with any other part of the anatomy would involve ducking the whole body, which is exactly what many unfortunate players do owing to this mistaken advice. We don't need to consider the consequences of this.

There is the same objection to starting the forward swing with the arms as there is to starting the backswing that way—*i.e.,* the movable hub—as well as all the other factors mentioned when describing the golf secret.

I will say again that with iron clubs the ball is hit as the club head comes down, simply because impact occurs before the club head reaches the bottom of its arc, but the swing with irons is exactly the same as with woods—upward.

Pull-down-with-left-arm. This is a commonly advised wrong method of beginning the forward swing.

It is to be deprecated along with hitting down with irons and for the same reasons.

Don't do it. Concentrate on your left shoulder and swing upward.

Hitting Late. Perhaps I should say a little here for the benefit of the arm hitters, and more later under "Hands" for the hand hitters.

I will say, first of all, that they are both wrong. Concentrate on the left shoulder, then the arms and hands will come in automatically. There is perhaps some advantage in assisting the left shoulder by active use of the right upper arm, but this is quite different from hitting late with the arms.

This so-called hitting at the correct time will occur automatically, at the correct time to suit the individual player, if the forward swing is executed mainly by the left shoulder and is therefore rhythmical.

The term "hitting area," like many other golfing expressions, does more harm than good and should be scrapped. In its place should be used the correct definition of that position in the forward swing. It should be described as the area before impact—which must vary with different players—where centrifugal force begins to increase the club-head speed and uncock the wrists, to enable the hands and the club head to pass the body and thus attain their maximum speed soon after impact.

You should actually be hitting from the very commencement of the forward swing, which you begin with the left shoulder. This body movement, initiated by the left shoulder, should be uninterruptedly completed as quickly as possible. Momentum (not you) will naturally, gradually, and rhythmically increase the speed of the swing and of the club head until centrifugal force takes over. But you must not interfere by some futile extra hitting—either late or early—somewhere in the middle of the effort.

Think of the boy throwing a stone. Does he think of hitting late? No! Does the whip-cracker think of

GOLF FALLACIES—IN TRUE LIGHT 117

hitting late? No! Does the boxer think of hitting late? No!

All these performers think of hitting from the moment they start the backswing. Their abstract thought becomes a concrete action from the moment they start the forward swing.

So it is with all similar activities, including golf.

USE AND MISUSE OF THE HANDS

This involves discussion of wrists and hands, loose grip, wrist-cocking, wrist-uncocking, wrist roll, open face and shut face, scooping, wrist flick, hitting late, hitting entirely with right hand, pull-down-with-left-hand, snatching, hands-first, swing-straight-back, club-head-close-to-ground, and swaying.

Wrists and Hands. The wrists have no strength, and no function other than to act as a hinge, therefore the wrist merely bends when the hand is used. We cannot use our wrists. The expression "wrists of steel" is merely the nonsense of fiction. The strength of the wrists is really the strength of the forearm muscles by means of which we move the hand and fingers, or grip.

Although you cannot keep your wrist firm unless you grip—*i.e.,* contract the forearm muscles—no matter how tightly you do it, it is still possible for your wrist to move freely. That fact—as fact it is—is contrary to the usual golf teaching that a tight grip prevents wrist work, and it proves that I am right in claiming that, no matter how tightly you grip, your wrists will function as and when they should. Prove that by clenching your right hand tightly and seeing how easily you can move your wrist.

The hands, when playing golf, merely grip or hold on to the club shaft. When that is done, they should be regarded as inseparably part of the shaft and nothing more—at any rate with all but the smallest of shots.

The muscles in the hands themselves are used chiefly for the more delicate finger work.

A good idea of wrist and hand function in the golf swing can be had by visualizing your left arm (shoulder to wrist) as a rod, and a golf club with your left hand fixed to it as another rod, your wrist being thought of as a hinge which connects the two rods together.

As the left shoulder goes down to begin the backswing, the wrist-hinge will be the first part to be pushed to the right (so-called hands-first); then centrifugal force will gradually swing the club head past the wrist (wrist-cocking). If the arm is now swung to the left by pulling the left shoulder upward (forward swing), the club and hand will continue to go to the right, thus continuing the cocking of the wrist-hinge. When the wrist is fully cocked, the rebound in conjunction with centrifugal force will start the wrist-uncocking, which will be complete at impact. At this stage, therefore, the arm and the hand attached to the club will be in one straight line.

Combined with the wrist-cocking and uncocking is a slight wrist roll, which can be appreciated by visualizing the arm being slightly rolled or twisted to the right during the backswing and to the left during the forward swing.

The reverse wrist-cocking and wrist roll after impact are not apparent for some distance owing to the fact that the arm, as well as the hand and club, is moving quickly onward.

It will now be apparent that the hands merely hold the club and that to obtain rhythm and good timing the wrist-cocking, wrist-uncocking, and wrist roll must all be automatic and subconscious and entirely the result of momentum and centrifugal force.

Loose Grip. I am sure that varying degrees of gripping with different fingers and with either hand, as often advocated, are not only unnecessary but undesirable. Lately, quite a number of professionals have advised a firmer grip, some with the left hand, some with both.

In my opinion, "holding on" at the top of the backswing, and firm contact with the ball at impact (both acknowledged to be essential), are only possible if the grip with all parts of both hands is very firm. This will not interfere with necessary wrist work.

Wrist-cocking. This, like other wrist movements, will occur automatically and to the varying extent necessary for different lengths of shot no matter how tightly you grip the club, providing you concentrate on your left shoulder and do not attempt to interfere by using your hands.

The cocking is entirely subconscious and is due to the momentum caused by the push-back of the club developing into a swing, plus centrifugal force.

Actually, it is probably best to forget all about wrist-cocking by gripping the club firmly and feeling, at the top of the swing, as though the wrists had not cocked. They will, despite your belief that you have prevented it, whereas if you try consciously to do it with your hands, you are sure to relax your grip, overswing, bend your left elbow, and probably lose control of the club.

Most high-handicap players swing further back than they think they do. Ask a friend to watch you do a full swing. Grip firmly and decide to finish the backswing with the club pointing to the sky. You will find that usually, in these circumstances, the club shaft goes nearer the correct horizontal than—as you thought—the perpendicular. The difference between your sensation and the fact is due to your inability to appreciate by means of your hands the effect of the momentum of the swing on the club head.

It is surprising how small an amount of wrist-cocking is possible in the average wrist. Address a ball; then, without permitting any movement above the wrists, raise the club head toward your face with your hands only. You will probably find that the left-index finger knuckle moves about one inch only, while the club head travels two or three feet—and that is without momentum!

It is that one inch that deceives you; therefore feel that it has not happened, and momentum will not only do it for you but will make it act as a powerful spring from which to rebound automatically on the forward swing.

Wrist-uncocking. All that has been said about wrist-cocking applies even more to wrist-uncocking. That is because there was no wound-up spring to begin the backswing and wrist-cocking, which there is for the forward swing and wrist-uncocking. Also, there is infinitely more momentum on the forward swing.

Uncocking of your wrists will occur automatically—and also of your left elbow—at the right time and place so long as you concentrate on your left shoulder traversing its groove, maintain a really firm grip with all parts of both hands, and don't interfere by trying to use your hands.

Wrist Roll. The first thing to say about this is that it has nothing at all to do with the wrists. It is the twisting of the forearms that changes our hands from palm down to palm up. Also, during a golf swing, there is a slight twist of the *upper* arm, without which the right elbow would not remain low down. Although wrist roll is performed by the arms, I am discussing it in this section because it is usually—though mistakenly—associated with the hands.

There should be no conscious wrist roll either on the backswing or on the forward swing. This belief appears to be at variance with the statement by some professionals that at or about impact the right hand turns sharply over the left; but what they don't explain is that this movement is absorbed into the rapid onward movement of the arms and hands and therefore is not apparent until later in the swing.

The fact is that the right hand crossing over the left is greatly an illusion, due to the simultaneous alteration in the position of the arms. Before impact the right elbow is much nearer the body—*i.e.,* further back than the left one—whereas after impact the left one moves further back.

There is undoubtedly some wrist roll in the golf swing, but it is only slight and entirely due to momentum. It will occur as and when it should automatically if you don't interfere by attempting to do it voluntarily.

Wrist-cocking and wrist-rolling, as well as wrist-uncocking and wrist-unrolling, are combined movements. To try consciously to improve on nature by increasing one or the other is comparable to throwing the proverbial monkey wrench into the works.

Open Face and Shut Face. There is definitely room for some clarification of this subject, especially with regard to the position at the top of the backswing.

Beyond stating that at the top of the backswing when the club face faces front the club face is open, and when it faces the sky it is shut, most professionals fight shy of the subject. I disagree with these definitions and believe that in both instances the face is open, the difference being one of degree. I will go further and say that a shut-faced position of the club at the top of a golf swing is a physical impossibility. The nearest approach to it is the swing of James Bruen, who carries his right elbow very high in the backswing; but even so, by means of a loop, his forward swing becomes more orthodox.

Let us see what opens and shuts the club face.

Address a ball; then, without any wrist roll, make the club head describe a quarter of a circle, on the ground,

GOLF FALLACIES—IN TRUE LIGHT 123

around your right leg. Now, although the club shaft points to your right and the club face faces directly forward, it has not opened because your arms, hands, and the club head still have the same relationship as at the address.

Again address the ball, and then, without swinging, open, then shut, the club face. You had to roll your wrists to the right to open the face and to the left to shut it. Remember that during the golf swing it is involuntary wrist roll that opens and shuts the club face.

Of course I know that, if it were possible from the address position to carry the club head to the top with its face at right angles to the target line all the way, the face would then face the sky and that would be an extreme shut-face swing. But that is a physical impossibility and therefore proves nothing.

Will the reader attempt that swing now. He will find that he can get his hands only about shoulder high and that the club must remain in front of him; also—and this is important—his wrists have rolled to the left, and the back of his left hand faces the ground. But, on any backswing that is physically possible, even before the hands are shoulder high and even in the so-called shut-faced swing that makes the club face at the top face the sky, the back of the left hand faces mainly to the sky.

Surely that is proof of wrist roll to the right and of a consequent open face!

I am sure there has been too much made of the difference between the English open-faced swing and the so-called new American shut-faced swing, which, as I have shown, are both open-faced, the difference being only one of degree.

Almost all photographs of experts—American and British—halfway through the backswing show, as above described, the club head pointing backward and the club face partly facing the sky. The degree varies with different people, as also does the level at which the face-opening begins; for example, if the club head moves last, the wrist roll and face-opening will be thereby delayed.

At least one of the notable modern American so-called shut-faced-swing school—whose photographs show what I have just described—says that on the backswing the club face neither shuts nor opens. Other people say it shuts; I have just *proved* that it opens. We must not always accept expert opinions in golf or in anything. They often differ and are often wrong.

From that halfway position to the top of the backswing, the toe of the club head leads and ultimately swings toward your back, stopping with the club face in some degree facing the sky.

Now, this club-face position at the top has nothing at all to do with the so-called open-faced or shut-faced swinging. The degree to which it faces the sky is influenced by the grip—*i.e.,* the more the left hand is on top of the shaft, the more the club face faces the sky. But the real factor is the position of the hands at the top of the backswing. The further back the hands, the more the club face faces the sky. This can be seen by comparing professionals' photographs. In addition, the further back the hands, the more the right wrist—

GOLF FALLACIES—IN TRUE LIGHT

and elbow—are under the shaft. Note this well: that is *why* the left hand is more in front of the shaft and with less wrist cock.

This far-back position of the hands may be influenced by long arms, but the chief factor in permitting it is a low left shoulder—as previously described—at the top of the backswing. The player must not attempt to push his hands backward; they go into that position automatically as he pushes his left shoulder down and his left upper arm up.

If the reader will put himself into the top of the swing position just described and then deliberately cock his left wrist more—watching it—he will see that the back of his left hand to some extent comes toward the back of his forearm, which movement will cause the club face to face less to the sky.

He may find it difficult to cock the left wrist more unless he brings his hands a little forward. This apparently small fact provides the key to those cases in which the club face at the top of the swing is facing forward. The club face is in that position, and the toe is pointing to the ground, when the hands are less far back, so that the club shaft is more above the shoulder, nearer the neck. In addition, in these cases, the right elbow is usually a little backward and higher, whereas the left wrist is more under the shaft, and with more cocking and a longer backswing.

That is the real and only difference between the so-called shut-faced and open-faced positions at the top. Briefly, when the hands are well back, the left wrist is more to the front and there is less left-wrist-cocking—

therefore the club face in some degree faces the sky—whereas when the hands are less far back, the left wrist is more under the shaft and there is more left-wrist-cocking—therefore the club face faces the front. This explanation accounts for all the intermediate positions of the club face with different players.

Notable examples of the top-of-the-swing position with the club face facing the front (and hands less far back) are Bobby Jones, Leonard Crawley, and Percy Alliss in his younger days. (I haven't seen any recent photographs of Percy Alliss at the top of the swing.)

This brings us to the conclusion that there is no such thing as a correct open-faced swing or correct shut-faced swing, because the former would require voluntary wrist roll, while the latter would require voluntary inhibition of the natural automatic wrist roll—both incorrect because wrist roll should be involuntary.

If the backswing is performed as described, the correct position at the top will be inevitable; then, when the forward swing is begun by pulling the left shoulder upward, the club head, when about halfway down, will be in some degree behind the player; while the toe will be in some degree pointing backward and the club face in some degree facing the sky. This position of the club head and club face is proof that the club face is still open.

Again, as on the backswing, this position of the club head and face on the forward swing can be seen in photographs of most American or British experts.

From this position, the continued upward movement of the left shoulder into its half-circle groove will carry the club face "square to the line" at impact and for a considerable distance beyond because the reverse wrist roll is delayed.

The after-impact position of the club face is further discussed in the next section.

Scooping. Professionals always say, "Don't scoop." Scooping, as I understand it, is striking the ball and allowing the club head to follow it with the face square to the target, but at the same time leaving the hands behind at impact position; or worse still, raising the hands as though to lift, instead of loft, the ball.

That, of course, is bad, but there is nothing wrong with the club-head position if the hands also travel onward. Indeed it is very desirable and is proof that the shot has been hit upward, since in many cases it has the effect of bending the back of the left hand toward the forearm. This hingelike bending of the left wrist is plainly shown in many photographs of first-class golfers, both with short and long clubs.

That square club face for a considerable distance after impact, with or without the left-wrist hinging, is the natural consequence of the swing that I advocate; and it is typical of the so-called American shut-faced swing, as well as of the swings of many British experts, thus bearing out my belief that the difference between the American and British swings is merely one of degree.

The possibility of the above-described hingelike action of the left wrist renders wrist work even more complicated and suggests that the player who tries to find the combination of wrist-uncocking, wrist-rolling, and wrist-hinging, to suit him is making a grave mistake.

I think that, provided the swing is executed correctly and always the same way, the right combination of these wrist actions for the individual player will occur automatically and will depend chiefly on whether the swing tends to be upright or flat. The flatter the swing, the more the wrist roll. The more upright the swing, the more the hinge movement—or no wrist movement at all, until the wrist roll becomes apparent later.

Since my thesis is based on a horizontal upper part of the spine producing an upright swing, I must plump for no wrist movement at all soon after impact, unless it be a little hingelike action.

Wrist Flick. This is really the same as wrist roll and is sometimes referred to as the flick at the bottom of the swing.

It is a dangerous conception, for it encourages a quick opening and shutting of the club face by the hands, with as many possible directions for the ball to travel as there are tangents to a circle. It is another expression and idea best forgotten.

Maybe instead of the flick being achieved by a wrist roll, a wrist-hinging is advocated, as mentioned under "Scooping." Any method of flicking with the hands should be taboo, as the function of the hands is merely to grip the club. The only flick that is necessary is the subconscious uncocking of the wrist.

Hitting Late. As with the arms, hitting late with the hands implies making an extra effort in the middle of

GOLF FALLACIES—IN TRUE LIGHT

the forward swing. Could anything be more calculated to upset rhythm?

Again, hitting late with the hands envisages a voluntary uncocking of the wrists part way down, but wrist-uncocking should be involuntary and the automatic result of the rebound from wrist-cocking, which is not complete until the forward swing is under way.

Therefore, with a correct swing induced by the left shoulder, all that is implied by the misleading expression "hitting late" will occur automatically.

You should feel that you are hitting from the start of the forward swing—*i.e.,* early!

Hitting Entirely with the Right Hand. At least one expert advocates doing this when playing a full shot. It seems to me, and it has been my experience when trying the method, that a full shot played entirely right-handed holds the weight back, with obvious undesirable consequences.

I also feel that those who think they do this have so well trained the left side of the body that it functions without their knowledge.

I have already discussed the possibility of right-handed play with short shots, but even with these, starting with the left side appears to be desirable, to ensure the rhythmic flow of whatever weight should go into the shot.

Lastly, I would condemn hitting with the right hand just as I would hitting with the left hand because the function of both hands is only to grip.

The hit is assisted by the right arm, not hand.

Pull-down-with-the-left-hand. What I have said about pulling down with the left arm also applies to the hand, only more so.

It is pulling on the middle of the rope. Also it must start to undo the wrist-cocking, since you cannot use your hand without wrist movement in the same direction. Even worse, you will be undoing the wrist-cocking before it is complete, since the wrist should be still in the process of cocking after the forward swing has well begun. Lastly, thinking of the hand at all is more likely than anything else to cause snatching. Therefore forget it.

Snatching. I believe that much the commonest cause of this is pulling down with the left hand or arm. The only other possible cause is anxiety to hit the ball, and this will not cause snatching if the forward swing is commenced with the left shoulder.

Hands-first. The conception of this is correct only in so far as the hands should begin to move before the club head, although the start may be so slight as to be almost imperceptible. That is the reason why some say hands before club head, while others say both together. The important thing is that there should be no wrist-cocking at this stage.

But the left hand should not be the first part of the anatomy to move. The left shoulder going down pushes the left arm to the right, causing the wrist to bend slightly backward and move to the right before the hand.

To perform hands-first by means of the hand or hands would tend to make the shoulder, and therefore the head, also move to the right—*i.e.,* to sway. These are natural consequential movements to be expected in such circumstances.

Think only of the left shoulder, and the hand and the club head will move correctly.

Swing-straight-back. The experts often say, "Start the backswing by swinging the club head straight back." They variously say, "on the reverse target line," "for the first few inches," "six to eight inches," "about a foot," or "a foot or so."

Deliberately attempting to get any of these distances will tend to make you look to see if it is happening and also make the whole body sway to the right.

Actually, the flatter the swing, and consequently the more inclined the plane of the *club-head* arc, the shorter will be the distance that the club head remains on that straight line. Conversely, the more upright the swing, the more upright the plane of the club-head arc, and therefore the longer will the club head travel straight behind the ball.

But, as previously stated, by starting the backswing by depressing the left shoulder and feeling that you are swinging the club head straight up, it will automatically go straight back behind the ball for the necessary distance.

In this instance again, people confuse what they should do, with what happens in consequence of doing something else.

Club-head-close-to-the-ground. In conjunction with "straight back," goes the instruction to keep the club head close to the ground. Both have the same consequences, as described; also, both tend to keep the left shoulder high and to restrict the shoulder pivot.

Particularly is this the case with club-head-close-to-the-ground because the player, uncertain as to when to let it come up, may let the club head swing around his right leg like a scythe. Perhaps that fault would be partly corrected during the course of the swing if it always happened the same. But—and this is important—it would never be twice the same; the backswing, therefore, would vary, especially with different clubs, and would never get into anything approaching a groove.

Once again then, left-shoulder-down will not only ensure the club head's going straight back, but straight back close to the ground—and automatically for the correct distance.

Swaying. Embryo golfers are always told not to sway, and rightly so, but how can they avoid it if they are also told to do the aforementioned things that cause it?

Swaying implies a lateral movement of the head alternately to right and left. It is important to realize that this is a perfectly natural movement when playing a shot, visualized as a backswing straight to the right and a hit straight to the left. Take the example of a tennis player: as he swings back in preparation for, say, a forehand drive, his head moves to the right with the rest of his body, then to the left as he strikes. That is where golf appears to be unnatural. But it becomes natural enough if you do an upright swing by revolving the shoulders around a horizontal upper part of the spine, and thus keep the head, like a turnip on a spike, in the same position during the entire swing, until the ball has been dispatched.

That is why I maintain that the feel of the swing, as distinct from what happens automatically, should be merely up to the right and up to the left.

I would again stress the fact that the head not only can, but should, turn right or left on its own axis, as much as it—or its owner—likes.

Use and Misuse of the Fairway

This involves a study of divots and ball position, and since they are inseparable, they will be considered together.

Divots and Ball Position. Divots are of two kinds, intentional and unintentional. The former are usually considered desirable, and are taken in front of the ball after it has been hit; the latter are definitely undesirable and are taken behind the ball before it has been hit.

The length and depth of any divot depends on how far behind the bottom of its arc the club head contacts the ground, whereas if the club head contacts the ground exactly at the bottom of its arc, there will be no divot. For our present purposes we can ignore any flattening of the bottom of the arc.

What happens to the ball will depend on whether it is in front of, at, or behind the bottom of the arc. See Diagram 13, in which the letters mark the sections of the diagram as well as the club shaft, while the arrows indicate the direction of the forward swing.

A represents a clean shot with no divot, the hands

being above the ball, which is the normal position at the bottom of the swing arc.

B represents an intentional small shallow divot, the hands being slightly ahead of the ball, which is therefore to the right. The ground was struck in front of— *i.e.,* after—the ball.

C represents an intentional large deep divot, the hands being well ahead of the ball, which is therefore still nearer the right foot. Again the ground was struck in front of, or after, the ball.

D represents an unintentional divot caused by the hands being too near the ball, and due to either standing too near the ball or using a club that is too long. In either case the ground is struck behind—*i.e.,* before— the ball. Incidentally, being too near the ball is probably also the commonest cause of shanking, hitting the ball with the neck of the club.

E represents an unintentional divot, the ball being in the normal no-divot position, with the hands above it at address. This divot is due to some fault keeping the weight back on the right leg and consequently also keeping the hands and the arc back so that the ground is struck behind—*i.e.,* before—the ball, which is topped.

F represents an intentional divot, the hands being ahead of the ball, which is nearer the right foot and in a cuppy-lie—*i.e.,* it is partly under the ground. Theoretically, the ball should always be struck before the ground, but when the ball is partly submerged, it might require too steep a blow to dislodge it, necessitating the ball lying even to the right of the right foot. In this case, it seems to me to be geometrically correct to play

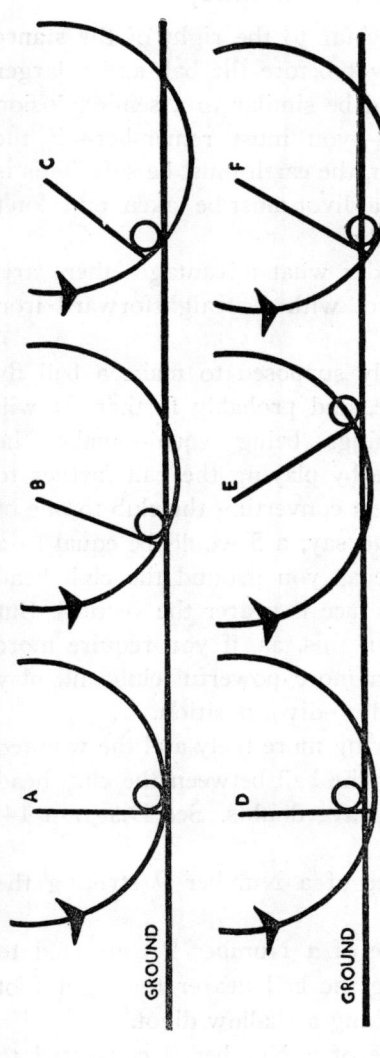

DIAGRAM 13. DIVOTS

A divot is the earth removed by the club head, after impact with the ball if intentional, before impact if unintentional. In the diagram, the line connecting the letters A to F to the ball represents arms and club: A—Hands above ball; no divot. B—Hands ahead of ball; small divot. C—Hands further ahead of ball; large divot. D—Hands above but too near the ball (many reasons); unintentional divot. E—Weight too far to right at impact; unintentional divot, followed by topped ball. F—Hands ahead of ball to extract partly submerged ball; two intentional divots—small one before, and large one after impact.

Are divots necessary? Harry Vardon didn't think so. George Duncan doesn't. Therefore I am in good company! See text, for and against.

the ball only reasonably far to the right of the stance and to take a small divot before the ball and a larger one after it. This would be similar to a semiexplosion shot from sand, since—you must remember—if the ball is stuck in the earth, the earth must be soft. This is the only instance when a divot must be taken, and don't forget to grip very firmly.

We must now consider what advantages there are, if any, in taking a divot with a straightforward iron shot.

To do so is generally supposed to make a ball fly straight and more true, and probably further. It will undoubtedly—other things being equal—make the ball go further, because by playing the ball further to the right you are in effect converting the club to one of higher power. That is to say, a 5 would be equal to a 4 or even a 3, because as you ground the club head further to the right, its face is nearer the vertical. But there is no advantage in this, as, if you require more distance, you can use a more powerful club and play the ball from the normal no-divot position.

Regarding the ball flying more truly and the vaunted advantage of squeezing the ball between the club head and the earth, I have grave doubts. See Diagram 14, in which:

A represents the face of a Number 9 striking the ball with no divot.

B represents the face of a Number 9 converted to a Number 7 by playing the ball nearer the right foot with the intention of taking a shallow divot.

C represents the face of a Number 9 converted to

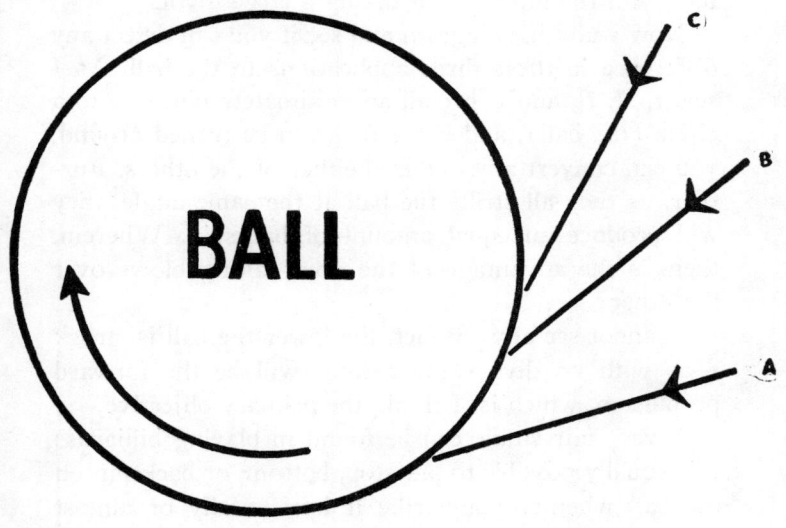

DIAGRAM 14. BACKSPIN

Backspin! The inevitable spin with which a golf ball travels when struck with any club except a straight-faced putter, provided no tee is used and ball is not topped. It is therefore unnecessary to make any effort to apply backspin. In the diagram, *A* represents Number 9 iron striking ball, with no divot; *B*—Number 9 converted to Number 7, ball further to the right, with intention of taking a divot; *C*—Number 9 converted to Number 5, ball still further to the right, with intention of taking larger divot. Where is the advantage of the divot-taking blows over the other, for, as the diagram shows, all three are tangents to a circle and must produce equal backspin? In fact, the advantage of the no-divot blow, which at impact will be more directly toward the target, should be a greater forward propulsion—the primary object!

a Number 5 by playing the ball still nearer the right foot with the intention of taking a large divot.

Now study the diagram and see if you can detect any difference in these three applications to the ball. As I see it, *A, B,* and *C* are all approximately tangents to a circle (the ball), and if the diagram be turned around, you can convert any one into either of the others. Further, as they all strike the ball at the same angle, they will produce an equal amount of backspin. Wherein, then, is the advantage of the divot-taking blows over the other?

I cannot see any. In fact, the lower the ball is struck —as with no divot—the greater will be the forward propulsion, which is, I think, the primary objective.

A very fair simile can be found in playing billiards: it is equally possible to put stop, bottom, or backspin on the ball whether you strike it horizontally or almost vertically, but the billiard ball will travel further if struck horizontally—which is comparable to no-divot.

So much for the "advantages" of taking a divot! What are the disadvantages? Briefly, the shot is made more difficult, more complicated, more varied, and less foolproof, as follows:

1. Playing the ball nearer the right foot necessitates adjustment of the grip.

2. The shaft will not be at right angles to the intended flight of the ball.

3. Standing a shade nearer the ball to allow for the bottom of the arc being under the earth.

4. A slight increase of body-bending to lower the hands.

GOLF FALLACIES—IN TRUE LIGHT

5. A tighter grip to counteract contact with the earth.

6. A likelihood of the club shaft turning in the hands at impact and causing a foul shot.

7. Because the ball is further to the right, the shot feels different and also looks different since you may be looking more at the front of the ball.

8. For the reasons given in No. 7 you may hold the weight to the left or transfer too far to the right.

9. The human element of error may produce slight differences of contact with the ball, and consequently divots of different sizes and different resistances to the blow.

10. The resistance will further differ with the condition of the ground, which may be harder or softer even on the same course and therefore during the course of one round.

I am forced to the conclusion—and it has been my experience—that it is much easier, more consistent, and no disadvantage to play straightforward iron shots with the ball in the normal no-divot position at the bottom of the arc.

Admittedly, most professionals take divots, but some, notably George Duncan and the late Harry Vardon—than whom there has probably never been a better golfer—have thought them unnecessary. What proved better for these great players will surely prove better for many lesser players; and it is possible that many professionals have slavishly accepted and followed the divot-taking dictum of others without proving its advantages or otherwise.

However, each player should find for himself which method suits him better, and then, except in exceptional circumstances, stick to it.

One final word about divots: if you must take them, replace them.

Chapter 5

COORDINATION OF THE THREE FACTORS—WITH OTHER DETAILS

Shape of the Body
Feel of the Swing
Backswing
Forward Swing
Postscript
Quintessence

SHAPE OF THE BODY

Regarding the shape of your spine, and consequently, of course, your back, always have the upper part of it about horizontal; and feel that you are facing the top of the ball, that it is under the upper part of your body rather than in front of you, and that you are looking down at it with wide-open eyes.

With the ball somewhere opposite the left half of your body, you will then be looking, as you should be, at the top back of it.

Your back has to be bent the appropriate amount, until the club head rests on the ground. Do not make the mistake of applying the club head to the ground by increasing the angle that your hands, and therefore also the club shaft, make with your arms. (Do not misunderstand what is meant by "increasing the angle." The angle is increased when it is less apparent, because then the arms and the club shaft are more nearly in a straight line.)

You can guard against that by remembering that your arms should be hanging straight down perpendicularly, at least with the short and medium length clubs. Even with the long clubs the arms should be almost perpendicular, the hands being only slightly more forward than the shoulders, and never reaching forward.

Think of your head as being not above your shoulders but in front of them and facing downward; and think of your shoulders and arms as being in front of your legs. Don't think of an upright body with arms and club sticking forward.

Those are the details of the forward curve of the body, but remember that there is also a lateral curve to the left. Remember that that is due entirely to the right hand being lower than the left one on the shaft of the club.

If you play the ball opposite the left half of your body, which this hand position demands, then you will assume that shape, or set, of the body quite naturally. You must not try any tricks such as "placing" your left shoulder or right knee. If you do so you will overdo the lateral curve.

Feel of the Swing

So far as your conscious feelings are concerned, always visualize the golf swing, back and forward, as essentially an almost perpendicular revolving of the

COORDINATION OF THE THREE FACTORS 143

shoulders around an almost horizontal upper part of the spine.

That is simplicity itself, and if you remember it, you cannot go far wrong.

When you stand erect, the upper part of the spine of course practically perpendicular, a golf swing would be around the body, but the club head at impact would be two or three feet above the ground. But when the back is correctly bent so that the upper part of the spine is practically horizontal, although you still swing identically around the upper part of the spine, the feeling in, and the effects upon, all that part of the body below the chest is entirely different.

In the former case the feeling was entirely of rotation and swinging in a consequently flat circle. In the latter case, the feeling was of a left to right, then right to left movement, and of swinging in a consequent "straight" line, more or less.

In actual fact it becomes almost a perpendicular circle, in other words, an upright swing. Even in this latter event there is a rotation of the lower part of the body, but it is secondary to what you do with your shoulders, and therefore it is not impressed on your consciousness—*i.e.,* it is a subconscious movement.

There is a subtle difference between these two swings. When you swing rotatorily, or flat, the whole body is moving in the same direction; therefore there is no check, or brake, at the top of the backswing, and consequently you tend to lose your balance. On the other hand, when you rotate the upper part of your body vertically around a horizontal axis (the upper part of the spine), this causes the lower part of the body, after a slight lateral shift, to rotate horizontally around a more or less vertical axis (the lower part of spine).

It is the fact that these two rotations—one voluntary and vertical, the other involuntary and horizontal—act as a check, or brake, on each other near their completion that renders the very important balance not only automatic but inevitable.

As the shoulders are revolved around the upper part of the spine during the execution of the backswing, the left arm and the club go up and also back. I would stress that this backward movement is not deliberate; in fact, it is an illusion. This illusion is entirely due to the subconscious turning of the lower part of the body carrying the shoulders and the club around to the right. The feeling was merely left shoulder down and left upper arm up. At the top of the backswing, the left arm is still, as it must be, in front of the upper part of the body.

Exactly the same thing occurs, and the same feeling is experienced, on the forward swing after impact.

Backswing

The backswing is commenced by pushing the left shoulder down, which has the effect of setting the hub of the swing (the upper part of the spine) in motion. At the same time or immediately afterward, the left hand with the club is pushed upward by the left-shoulder muscles acting on the upper arm. The push soon changes to a swing.

COORDINATION OF THE THREE FACTORS 145

These two movements occur simultaneously or practically so, and are complementary. That is to say, each helps the other. The shoulder going down helps the arm and the club to go up; and the arm going up ensures the shoulder going well down and then to the right. These combined movements also ensure that there is a full shoulder pivot and that the hands holding the club are well back, in line with the tip of the right shoulder, at the top of the backswing.

While you have in the above simple manner executed a perfect backswing, many other things have occurred automatically:

1. You thought only of the left side, but the right arm assumed its natural and correct position. The right upper arm remained near your body until late in the swing; then, if the swing were long enough to need it, it was involuntarily lifted off your body by the swing, the elbow still pointing more or less downward.

2. As the left shoulder went down, the right one went up, and the hands traveled to the right on the same level as at the address: consequently, for the first foot or so the club head traveled straight back to the right close to the ground.

3. As the shoulders gradually turned, ultimately to make the chest face to the right, so were the arms and the club carried around appearing to swing on an inclined plane. This shoulder-turning, you will remember, was due to the automatic rotation of the pedestal, or lower part of the body. The inclined-plane illusion was augmented by the subconscious arm-twisting to the

right, which occurred in conjunction with the similarly subconscious wrist-cocking.

At this point I had better admit the obvious: that even with an upright swing as described, the club head (note well that I said club head, not your hands) does swing on an inclined plane, but that is no concern of the player's! His sensation is of swinging his arms, more or less in a straight line. That is why I call it an inclined-plane illusion. Your sensations and feelings are entirely in your own body and not in the wood and steel of the club.

Of course you can always tell, by the position of your hands, the place and angle of the club head; but the professionals' admonition to be aware of the position of the club head has a lot to answer for.

4. When you approached the top of the backswing, with the club face having been gradually opened by the slight, natural, involuntary twisting of the forearms to the right, the club shaft was pointing backward and to the sky in a line parallel to the club shaft at address position.

Here again, you must not *swing* into that position. It occurs automatically owing to the involuntary rotation of the pedestal and the involuntary forearm twist, which also cause the back of the left hand to face somewhat to the sky.

5. When the shoulders completed their pivot, the hands were in line with the right shoulder, over which the club shaft was shortly to be pointing to the target, by which time the wrists would have almost completed their automatic cocking.

6. Your weight transferred, exactly as much as it should have, without any conscious help from you.

7. In the meantime, the right hip went backward and the left one forward; the left knee bent, and the left foot rolled on to its inside edge with a tendency for the heel to rise.

You have now completed the backswing—what little you had to do—and all the subconscious occurrences have happened. Your head is in its original position slightly turned to the right, or has been turned there by the late stages of the shoulder pivot; you are looking down at the top back of the ball; you feel perfectly balanced; you are ready to begin the forward swing while the wrists are still cocking.

Forward Swing

Briefly, on any full shot your thoughts from the very beginning of the forward swing should be of speed and of hitting upward with all you've got, remembering to maintain a firm grip with all parts of both hands and to "see the ball hit."

Soon after "thinking" you have seen the ball hit, your shoulders will twist your neck and compel your head to turn to the left.

You will have exactly the same sensations with the irons as with the woods, and also even with an explosion shot from a bunker. The iron shots will be downward hits even though you are hitting upward, because the ball, being further to the right, will be contacted by the club head as it comes down, and before it has reached, or at any rate passed, the bottom of the arc.

We have already discussed the disastrous consequences of really hitting down.

The first and most important thing to think of—in fact, maybe the only thing—is the left shoulder, which you pull up as quickly as you can the moment it has momentarily stopped on completion of *its* backswing. You will remember that at that moment the remainder of the backswing (of arm, hand, and club head) is not quite complete.

In performing its half circle, the left shoulder must first go to the left, then up, and finally to the right behind your neck. The upward movement is the one that is apt to be forgotten and at the same time is the most important, because it ensures the left shoulder's being high and both shoulders being square to the line at impact instead of turned to the left.

While the left shoulder is leading the forward swing into the groove, several things happen automatically without any assistance from you:

1. Your weight is transferred to the left.

2. Your left hip goes backward out of the way.

3. Your left foot goes flat on to the ground, and the left leg becomes firm.

4. Your arms, with the wrist now fully cocked, and the club head trailing behind, are involuntarily brought down in their correct relative positions—*i.e.,* the right elbow close to your body, and the left arm further away from you—into the so-called hitting area, thus ensuring the normal inside-to-out swing.

5. In a flash, the wrists involuntarily uncock, and the club head makes solid contact with the ball, which

COORDINATION OF THE THREE FACTORS 149

travels straight down the middle. Meanwhile, the hands travel straight on without stopping, and so quickly that the crossing over of the hands (reverse wrist roll) appears to be delayed until well into the so-called follow-through.

6. The back-bending and the intention to hit upward prevent the head from being pulled up, but when the right shoulder is nearly under the chin, your twisted neck turns your head to the left.

7. The momentum from hitting upward ensures the club head's following the ball and traveling its fastest after impact—which most experts agree it should. This also makes what is mistakenly called hitting late inevitable though involuntary. Also, a full follow-through and a high finish are ensured since you actually hit into them.

8. Meanwhile, the right hip automatically comes forward, causing the right foot to roll on to its inside edge and finally more or less on to its toe as the entire weight moves on to the firm left leg.

You have now completed the forward swing—what little you had to do—and all the subconscious occurrences have happened.

Now while a thoroughly efficient forward swing can be performed by thinking only of the left shoulder as above described, it would be fatuous of me to suggest that your very powerful shoulder muscles cannot assist the shot by swinging the upper arms.

With the intention to hit upward, I am convinced, these muscles will function to some extent automatically; and what is more, at the right time and place, since you cannot hit upward with your arms until they have come down into the accepted hitting area. Remember that they come down that far automatically in consequence of the body movement initiated by the left shoulder, so that by the time your thought of hitting is transformed into action, you are in a position to hit upward.

Therefore I would suggest that, after you have mastered what we will call the left-shoulder-up forward swing, you then try voluntarily to assist it by swinging your upper arms with your shoulder muscles.

If you can time this action correctly, you should gain extra length.

With the intention to hit upward "with all you've got" firmly in your mind, begin the forward swing by pulling your left shoulder upward as quickly as possible.

Immediately that movement has started, hit upward with your right upper arm (not your hand), leaving the left-shoulder muscles to come into the shot automatically, which they will do because your mind is already on your left shoulder.

With practice you may acquire the feeling of the left shoulder and the right arm, as above described, beginning the forward swing simultaneously. But if you try too soon to do it that way, you may find that sometimes the right arm will get in first, before the left shoulder has determined the groove. In that case you would probably not transfer your weight properly to the left, and in consequence would have both heels off the ground at impact; or worse, you would take a divot before contacting the ball; or worse still, top the ball or miss it altogether.

Never forget that it is the left shoulder going upward that produces the desirable grooved swing. Nothing must supersede that.

When using the right arm in the manner described, I know that some people will feel that they are hitting with their right forearm or hand, but I am certain that it is the upper arm, activated by the powerful shoulder muscles, that should be thought of and cultivated in hitting the ball, because that method, by swinging the whole arm correctly from its top end, keeps the arm straight, thus ensuring a wide swing. The action could be likened to the boxer's straight left from the shoulder.

Postscript

To avoid any possibility of misunderstanding, we will examine three important items—metaphorically—under the microscope.

1. I have repeatedly stated that a golf shot should be a straight-line shot and have emphasized that the left shoulder and the hands feel to be traveling in a straight line. That is to say, the left shoulder goes straight down, then straight up; and the hands go straight up to the right, then straight up to the left.

I used that expression deliberately in order to get away from the idea of swinging around the whole body. But you do swing around the upper part of the body; therefore, it is obvious that the degree of straightness of the swing will vary with the degree of back-bending.

The nearer the upper part of the spine is to the horizontal, the more upright will be the swing and the straighter the feeling of the shoulder and hand arcs.

2. The most important movement in the whole golf swing is that which begins the backswing; it is therefore desirable to have some means of checking its accuracy.

With the best intention in the world to begin by revolving the shoulders around the upper part of the spine, it is very easy to think you are doing so while in fact you are revolving your body around the lower part of the spine.

The best way to judge the correctness or otherwise of the backswing is by the nature of the forward swing after impact. That is what professionals mean when they say that a good follow-through and a high finish cannot influence the ball after it has gone, but that they are proof of the correctness of what happened before impact.

Having completed a swing, if you had the feeling after impact of hitting upward and then going to the left over your left shoulder, then the downward movement of the left shoulder on the backswing was correct. But if you felt that the forward swing after impact turned too much to the left—*i.e.,* too early, and consequently around any part of your body below the left shoulder, and therefore not sufficiently upward—that was because your left shoulder was not high enough at, and after, impact.

The reason the left shoulder was not high enough

COORDINATION OF THE THREE FACTORS 153

was that it did not go down perpendicularly enough on the backswing. Therefore, repeat the swing until you get sufficient downness on the backswing to produce sufficient upness on the forward swing.

I will anticipate criticism and agree that it would be reasonable to think that, if you turned the left shoulder forward toward the ball, the hands and the club shaft would finish further back than if you pushed the shoulder downward. Reasonable though it may seem, it is quite wrong.

If you turn the shoulder toward the ball, the left heel will come up too far and balance will be insecure; therefore, the shoulder pivot will be incomplete, and at the top of the backswing the club shaft will probably be above your neck and pointing to the left of the target.

Conversely, if you push the left shoulder straight down, the left foot will roll on to its inside edge, the heel rising but slightly, your balance will be good, you will get a full shoulder pivot, and at the top of the backswing the club shaft will be above the tip of your right shoulder—or even further back—and pointing to the target.

Compare those two shoulder movements—don't take my word for it!

3. I have discussed the part that the arms play in the golf swing and admitted the possibility of their voluntary use. All the same I believe that a majority of golfers will get better results—except maybe in the short shots—if they forget all about their arms (except to grip firmly) and concentrate entirely on the left

shoulder, but remember to move it through a full half circle to behind the neck. It is that *quick half circle* that gives power and length.

In this event, don't imagine that your arms, through your shoulder muscles, are doing nothing. They will probably do more subconsciously, and certainly with more accurate timing, than you could do with them consciously.

I will again anticipate criticism by saying that it is because so much of the golf swing is automatic that golf professionals hold such divergent views as to whether golf is a right- or a left-handed game—or both.

For the same reason, their views are no less divergent on the subject of which part of the anatomy starts and continues both the backswing and the forward swing.

It is because professionals have overlooked the fact that most of the details of the golf swing are subconsciously performed that they are unable to analyze it accurately or with any degree of unanimity.

Quintessence

Apart from maintaining a firm grip, there are only four anatomical parts with which we are consciously concerned in executing the golf swing. They are the upper part of the spine, the left shoulder, and the left and right *upper* arms.

The first is used in *preparation* for the swing. The third and fourth can be left to themselves. The second is indispensable.

COORDINATION OF THE THREE FACTORS 155

Therefore the *left shoulder* is our sheet anchor. Whatever we forget, we must remember what to do with the left shoulder.

By this means we find ourselves with *one* point of concentration for the execution of the entire golf swing. And we also have the knowledge that we will *swing in the groove*.

That—in a nutshell—is *"The Golf Secret."*

INDEX

Accuracy of shot, 68
Address
  angles of, 26
  arm position at, 23
  head-turning at, 30
  position of, 20, 22, 25, 98
  spine at, 23
ALLISS, PERCY, 126
American swing, 123, 124, 127
Anatomy of spine, 29
Angles of address, 26
Arm
  hitters, 115
  movement
    conscious, 66, 68, 70, 96, 114, 153
    subconscious, 65, 68, 96
  position at address, 23
  speed, 74
  swing, direction of, 70

Back-bending, 20, 23, 25, 28, 33, 37, 60, 89, 100, 101, 103, 149, 151
Backswing
  beginning of, 41, 114
    with forearm, 42
    with hand, 42
    with left shoulder, 39, 45, 47, 90, 113, 144
    with upper arm, 42
  direction of left-shoulder movement during, 45
  effects of correct left-shoulder movement during, 49
  experts' contradictory beliefs about, 48
  meaning of, 85, 86, 87
  short, 23
  upper part of spine during, 31

Balance, 20, 36, 37, 61, 76, 103, 107, 108, 109, 143, 153
Ball
  and club head, 22, 114, 131
  position of, 133
  propulsion of, 138
  watching of, 20, 103, 141
Body
  ducking of, 115
  movement, 25, 82, 84
  shape of, 17, 20, 22, 89, 141
BRUEN, JAMES, 110, 122

Chip shots, 82
Club
  face
    loft of, 24, 59
    opening of, 33, 124, 146
  fit, 25
  head
    and ball, 22, 114, 131
    course of, 51
    and ground, 37, 73, 117, 131-2
    speed of, 74
  shaft
    length of, 20, 22, 23-4
    shortening of, 24
Cocking of wrists, 59, 92, 94-5, 96, 110, 118-21, 122, 130, 147, 148
Concentration, state of, 87-9
Conscious movement
  of arm, 66, 68, 70, 96, 114, 153
  in swing, 26, 36, 60, 62, 65, 71, 82
COTTON, HENRY, 110, 111
CRAWLEY, LEONARD, 126
Crouching, 25, 37, 98
Cuppy-lie, 134

INDEX

Daily Mail Tournament, 91
Direction of left-shoulder movement
  during backswing, 45
  during forward swing, 52
Divots, 133, 140, 151
Downswing, 71, 85, 86, 87
DUNCAN, GEORGE, 139

Effects of left-shoulder movement
  during backswing, 49
  during forward swing, 58
English swing, 123, 127
Exercises, 89, 97-100
Explosion shot, 81, 147

Feel of swing, 34, 37, 100, 133, 142
Finish, high, 68, 78, 110, 149, 152
Firm-left-leg, 104, 109, 148
Flat swing, 32-3, 89-90, 143
Follow-through, 52, 61, 77, 82, 85, 87, 149, 152
Forward press, 42, 103, 104-5, 109
Forward swing, 87, 89, 90, 147
  beginning of, 39, 51, 58, 80, 82, 90, 113, 115, 147
  direction of left-shoulder movement during, 52
  effects of correct left-shoulder movement during, 58
  experts' contradictory beliefs about, 56
  hands during, 22
  speed of shoulder movement during, 54

Golden Rule, 26, 47
Grip, 59, 66, 89, 99, 100, 110, 111, 113, 117, 118, 119, 124, 147, 154

Grooved swing, 45, 52, 53, 72, 73, 79, 83, 132, 148, 151, 155

Hands
  -first, 117, 118, 130
  during forward swing, 22
  use of, 117
Head
  -down, 100, 101
  -still, 100, 101
  -turning, 30, 100, 101, 132, 133
  -up, 30, 100, 101
Heel-raising, 74, 76, 103, 106, 109
Hip-turning, 63
Hitting
  area, 73, 80, 83, 116, 148, 150
  correct position for, 37
  down, 85, 86, 87, 110, 115
  hard, 91
  late, 110, 115, 117, 128-9, 149
  with right hand, 117, 129
  thinking of, 80
Holding-on, 119
Hubs of swing, 41, 63, 65, 95

Inside-to-out swing, 54, 74, 89, 90, 108, 148

JONES, BOBBY, 126

Knee
  -bending, 109
  placing of, 142

Left-heel-down, 104, 108, 109
Left-hip-back, 103, 107-8, 109
Left shoulder
  concentration on, 41, 45, 51, 61, 80, 83, 105, 115, 148, 155
  definition of, 40
  placing of, 142

INDEX

Left-side-out-of-the-way, 103, 108, 109
Left upswing, 86, 87
Leg-bending, 20
Lie, alteration of, 24
Limber-up, 62
LOCKE, BOBBY, 91
Loft of club face, 24, 59
Lurching, 86, 91

Mistiming, 97
Movement
  arm
    conscious, 66, 68, 70. 96, 114, 153
    subconscious, 65, 68, 96
  body, 25, 82, 84
  in swing
    conscious, 26, 36, 60, 62, 65, 71, 82
    subconscious, 26, 35, 36, 37, 38, 59, 60, 62, 82, 105, 109, 143, 148-50

No-divot position, 134, 136

Opening of club face, 33, 124, 146
Outside-to-in swing, 101

PICKWORTH, OSSIE, 109
Pivot, 103, 105-6, 109
Pivot, shoulder, 30, 31, 47, 82, 93, 98, 101, 106, 132, 145, 146
Placing
  of knee, 142
  of left shoulder, 142
Position
  of arm at address, 23
  of ball, 133
  for hitting, 37
  for no divot, 134, 136
Preparation for swing, 154

Pressing, 91
Propulsion of ball, 138
Pull-down
  -with-left-arm, 110, 115
  -with-left-hand, 117, 130
Pulling, 86
Putts, 81, 83, 94

Reaching forward, 142
Relaxation, 87-9
Rhythm, 80, 93, 95, 96, 97, 116, 119, 129
Right-elbow-down, 110-11

Scooping, 117, 127
Semiexplosion shot, 136
Set, 17, 25, 103, 104, 142
Shanking, 134
Short backswing, 23
"Short" game, 94
Short shots, 23, 81-3, 94-5, 106
Shoulder
  left
    concentration on, 41, 45, 51, 61, 80, 83, 105, 115, 148, 155
    definition of, 40
  pivot, 30, 31, 47, 82, 93, 98, 101, 106, 132, 145, 146
  placing of, 142
  -turning, 106, 145
Slicing, 44, 86, 101, 107
Snatching, 55, 117, 130
Speed
  of arm, 74
  of club head, 74
  of hand, 74
  of shoulder movement during forward swing, 54
  thinking of, 80, 147
Spine
  at address, 23
  anatomy of, 29
  -bending, 22

function of, 29
upper part of, 22, 26, 37, 38, 45, 46, 89, 90, 100, 101, 141, 143, 144, 152
vital part of, 22
Squeezing, 136
Stop at the top, 89, 91-5
Straight-left-arm, 110, 111-14
Straight-line shot, 55, 151
Subconscious movement
 of arm, 65, 68, 96
 in swing, 26, 35, 36, 37 38, 59, 60, 62, 82, 105, 109, 143, 148-50
Swaying, 33, 51, 71, 86, 117, 131, 132
Swing
 American, 123, 124, 127
 arm, direction of, 70
 back- (*see* Backswing)
 conscious movement in, 26, 36, 60, 62, 65, 71, 82
 English, 123, 127
 feel of, 34, 37, 100, 133, 142
 flat, 32-3, 89-90, 143
 forward (*see* Forward swing)
 grooved, 45, 52, 53, 72, 73, 79, 83, 132, 148, 151, 155
 hubs, 41, 63, 65, 95
 inside-to-out, 54, 74, 89, 90, 108, 148
 narrowing of, 67
 outside-to-in, 101
 points of pressure in, 93
 preparation for, 154
 shape of, 89, 90
 -straight-back, 117, 131
 subconscious movement in, 26, 35, 36, 37, 38, 59, 60, 62, 82, 105, 109, 143, 148-50
 upright, 28, 32-3, 89, 143, 146, 152
 wheel, 41
 wide, 68, 151

Synchronization, 66, 95, 96

Tension, 87-9
Timing, 66, 68, 89, 95, 96, 119, 150
Topping, 22, 55, 101, 151
Transfer of weight, 58, 70, 81, 83, 86, 97, 103, 106-7, 109, 147, 148, 150
Turn of the wrists, 34

Uncocking of wrists, 59, 95, 96, 117, 118, 121, 122, 129, 148
Upper part of spine, 22, 26, 37, 38, 45, 46, 89, 90, 100, 101, 141, 143, 144, 152
Upright swing, 28, 32-3, 89, 143, 146, 152
Upswing
 left, 86, 87
 right, 86

VARDON, HARRY, 111, 139

WARD, CHARLES, 91
Weight transfer, 58, 70, 81, 83, 86, 97, 103, 106-7, 109, 147, 148, 150
Wide swing, 68, 151
Wrist
 -cocking, 59, 92, 94, 95, 96, 110, 117, 118-21, 122, 130, 147, 148
 flick, 117, 128
 -hinging, 77, 118, 127, 128
 roll, 33, 77, 111, 117, 118, 119, 121-2, 123, 124, 128
 roll, reverse, 149
 -uncocking, 59, 95, 96, 117, 118, 121, 122, 129, 148
Wrists, 99, 110, 117, 118, 127

ZAHARIAS, BABE DIDRICKSON, 112